Fish of Missouri

FIELD GUIDE

by Dave Bosanko

Adventure Publications, Inc.
Cambridge, MN

ACKNOWLEDGEMENTS

Special thanks to the Dave Bierman from the Iowa Departmen of Natural Resources, for reviewing this book. Thanks are also due to the United States Fish and Wildlife Service and the Missouri Department of Natural Resources.

Edited by Brett Ortler

Cover and book design by Jonathan Norberg

Illustration credits by artist and page number:

Cover illustrations: Channel Catfish (main) and Bluegill (upper and ba cover) by Duane Raver/USFWS

Timothy Knepp/USFWS: 104 (main), 106 **MyFWC.com/fishing:** 12 **Dua Raver/USFWS:** 10 (bottom), 18, 22, 24, 26, 28, 30, 32, 34, 36, 38, 44, 4 48, 50, 52, 54, 56, 58, 68, 72, 90, 98, 108 (main), 110, 120, 122, 124, 12 146, 150, 152, 156, 158, 160, 162, 166, 170, 172, 176, 178, 180, 182, 1 **Joseph Tomelleri:** 40 (both), 42, 60, 62, 64, 66 (both), 70, 74 (both), 76, 7 80, 82 (all), 84, 86, 88, 92, 94 (both), 96, 100, 102, 104, 108 (both), 112 (all), 1 (both), 116, 118 (both), 126, 130, 132, 134, 136, 138, 140, 142, 144, 148, 15 164 (all), 168, 174, 184

Copyright 2013 by David Bosanko
Published by Adventure Publications, Inc.
820 Cleveland Street South
Cambridge, MN 55008
1-800-678-7006
www.adventurepublications.net
Printed in China

ISBN-13: 978-1-59193-264-2

TABLE OF CONTENTS

4

5

Silverside Family

Sturgeon Family

Sucker Family

Sunfish Family

Temperate Bass Family

HOW TO USE THIS BOOK

Your *Fish of Missouri Field Guide* is designed to make it easy to identify more than 80 species of the most common and important fish in Missouri and learn fascinating facts about each species' range, natural history and more.

The fish are organized by family, such as Catfish (Ictaluridae), Perch (Percidae), and Sunfish (Centrarchidae). Each family is then listed in alphabetical order. Within these families, individual species are arranged alphabetically in their appropriate groups. For example, members of the Sunfish family are divided into the Black Bass, Crappie and True Sunfish groups. For a detailed list of fish families and individual species, turn to the Table of Contents (page 3); the Index (page 192) provides a reference guide to fish by common name (such as goggle-eye) and other common terms for the species.

Fish Identification

Determining a fish's body shape is the first step to identifying it. Each fish family usually exhibits one or sometimes two basic outlines. Catfish have long, stout bodies with flattened heads, barbels or "whiskers" around the mouth, a relatively tall, but narrow, dorsal fin and an adipose fin. There are two forms of Sunfish: the flat, round, plate-like outline we see in Bluegills, and the torpedo or "fusiform" shape of Largemouth Bass.

In this field guide you can quickly identify a fish by first matching its general body shape to one of the fish family silhouettes listed in the Table of Contents (page 3). From there, turn to that family's section and use the illustrations and text descriptions to identify your fish. Sample Pages (page 22) are provided to explain how the information is presented in each two-page spread.

For some species, the illustration will be enough to identify your catch, but it is important to note that your fish may not look exactly like the artwork. Fish frequently change colors. Males that are brightly colored during the spawning season may show muted coloration at other times. Likewise, bass caught in muddy streams show much less pattern than those taken from clear lakes—and all fish lose some of their markings and color when removed from the water.

Most fish are similar in appearance to one or more other species—often, but not always, within the same family. For example, the Walleye is remarkably similar to the Sauger. To accurately identify such look-alikes, check the inset illustrations and accompanying notes below the main illustration, under the "Similar Species" heading.

Throughout *Fish of Missouri* we use basic biological and fisheries management terms that refer to physical characteristics or conditions of fish and their environment, such as dorsal fin or turbid water. For your convenience, these are listed and defined in the Glossary (page 188).

Understanding such terminology will help you make sense of reports on state and federal research, fish population surveys, lake assessments, management plans and other important fisheries documents.

FISH ANATOMY

To identify fish, you will need to know a few basic terms
that apply to fins and their locations.

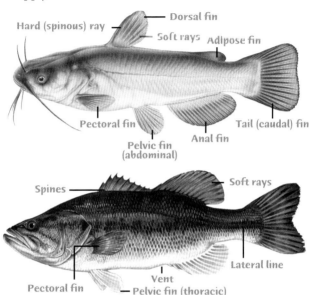

Fins are made up of bony structures that support a membrane. There are three kinds of bony structures in fins. **Soft
rays** are flexible fin supports that are sometimes branched.
Spines are stiff, often sharp, supports that are not jointed.
Hard rays are stiff, pointed, barbed structures that can be
raised or lowered. Catfish are famous for their hard rays,
which are mistakenly called spines. Sunfish have soft rays
associated with spines to form a dorsal fin.

Fins are named by their position on the fish. The **dorsal fin** is on the top along the midline. A few fish have another fin on their back called an **adipose fin**. This is a small, fleshy protuberance located between the dorsal fin and the tail and is distinctive of trout and catfish.

On each side of the fish near the gills are the **pectoral fins**. The **anal fin** is located along the midline on the fish's bottom or ventral side. There is also a paired set of fins on the bottom of the fish called the **pelvic fins**. Pelvic fins can be in the **thoracic position** just below the pectoral fins or farther back on the stomach in the **abdominal position**. The tail is known as the **caudal fin**.

Eyes—In general, fish have good eyesight. They can see color, but the light level they require to see well varies by species. For example, Walleyes see well in low light, whereas Bluegills have excellent daytime vision but see poorly at night, making them vulnerable to predation. Catfish have poor vision both night and day.

Nostrils—A pair of nostrils, or *nares*, is used to detect odors in the water. Eels and catfish have particularly well-developed senses of smell.

Mouth—The shape of the mouth is a clue to what the fish eats. The larger the food it consumes, the larger the mouth.

Teeth—Not all fish have teeth, but those that do have teeth designed to help them feed. Walleyes, northern pike and muskies have sharp *canine* teeth for grabbing and holding prey. Minnows have *pharyngeal* teeth—located in the throat—for grinding. Catfish have *cardiform* teeth, which feel like a rough patch in the front of the mouth. Bass have tiny patches of *vomerine* teeth in the roof of their mouths. **11**

Swim Bladder—Almost all fish have a swim bladder, a balloon-like organ that helps the fish regulate its buoyancy.

Lateral Line—This sensory organ helps the fish detect movement in the water (to help avoid predators or capture prey) as well as water currents and pressure changes. It consists of fluid-filled sacs with hair like sensors, which are open to the water through a row of pores in the skin along each side—creating a visible line along the fish's side.

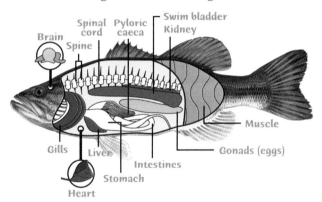

FISH NAMES

A Shellcracker is a Shellcracker in the south, but in the northern parts of its range it is called a Redear Sunfish. In other regions it's known as stumpknocker or yellow bream.

Because common names may vary regionally, and even change for different sizes of the same species, scientific names are used that are exactly the same around the world. Each species has only one correct scientific name that can be recognized anywhere, in any language. The Largemouth bass is *Micropterus salmoides* from St. Louis to Shanghai.

Scientific names are made up of Greek or Latin words that often describe the species. There are two parts to a scientific name: the generic or "genus," which is capitalized (*Micropterus*), and the specific name, which is not capitalized (*salmoides*). Both are displayed in italic text.

A species' genus represents a group of closely related fish. The Largemouth and Smallmouth bass are in the same genus, so they share the generic name *Micropterus*. But each fish has a different specific name, *salmoides* for Largemouth bass, *dolomieu* for the Smallmouth bass.

ABOUT FISH OF MISSOURI

Missouri is known for its many and varied rivers. It is bordered by the Mississippi and divided by the Missouri. In the north, slow, meandering streams like the Des Moines and Fox Rivers drain the prairies. Central and southern Missouri are renowned for the clear, cool streams of the Ozark Region. The Current River is one example; in 1964, it was designated as part of the Ozark National Scenic Riverways, the first national park established to protect a river system.

There are over 200 species of fish in Missouri. There is even a marine fish that migrates up the Mississippi River from the Gulf to spawn. Of these, over 80 species are represented in this book. About 40 of these fish are commonly targeted by anglers and another 40 or so are of interest to anyone that spends time near the water. Some of these fish are secretive and seldom seen, while others are commonly encountered, if only in the bait pail. All have interesting characteristics; learning about them will help you enjoy the time you spend around the water more.

FREQUENTLY ASKED QUESTIONS

What is a fish?

Fish are aquatic, typically cold-blooded animals that have backbones, gills and fins.

Are all fish cold-blooded?

All freshwater fish are cold-blooded. Recently, it has been discovered that some members of the saltwater Tuna family are warm-blooded. Whales and Bottlenose Dolphins are also warm-blooded, but they are mammals, not fish.

Do all fish have scales?

No. Most fish have scales that look like those on the Common Goldfish. A few, such as Alligator Gar, have scales that resemble armor plates. Catfish have no scales at all.

How do fish breathe?

A fish takes in water through its mouth and forces it through its gills, where a system of fine membranes absorbs oxygen from the water and releases carbon dioxide. Gills cannot pump air efficiently over these membranes, which quickly dry out and stick together. Fish should never be out of the water longer than you can hold your breath.

Can fish breathe air?

Some species can; gars have a modified swim bladder that acts like a lung. Fish that can't breathe air may die when dissolved oxygen in the water falls below critical levels.

How do fish swim?

Fish swim by contracting bands of muscles on alternate sides of their body so the tail is whipped rapidly from side to side. Pectoral and pelvic fins are used mainly for stability when a fish hovers, but are sometimes used during rapid bursts of forward motion.

Do all fish look like fish?

Most do and are easily recognizable as fish. The eels and lampreys are fish, but they look like snakes. Sculpins look like little goblins with bat wings.

Where can you find fish?

Some fish species can be found in almost any body of water, but not all fish are found everywhere. Each species has adapted to exploit a particular habitat. A species may move around within its home water, sometimes migrating hundreds of miles between lakes, rivers and tributary streams. Some movements, such as spawning migrations, are seasonal and very predictable.

Fish may also move horizontally from one area to another, or vertically in the water column, in response to changes in environmental conditions and food availability. In addition, many fish have daily travel patterns. By studying a species' habitat, food and spawning information in this book—and understanding how it interacts with other Missouri fish—

it is possible to make an educated prediction of where to find it in any lake, stream or river.

FISH DISEASES

Fish are susceptible to various parasites, infections and diseases. Some diseases have little effect on fish populations, while others may have a devastating impact. While fish diseases can't be transmitted to humans, they may render the fish inedible. To prevent the spread of such diseases, care should be taken in not transferring diseased fish from one body of water to another. Information on freshwater fish diseases in Missouri can be found at the Missouri Department of Conservation website, www.mdc.mo.gov.

INVASIVE SPECIES

While some introduced species have great recreational value, many exotic species have caused problems. Never move fish, water or vegetation from one lake or stream to another, and always follow state laws. Details about Invasive Species are available at Missouri Department of Conservation website, www.mdc.mo.gov.

FUN WITH FISH

There are many ways to enjoy Missouri's fish, from reading about them in this book to watching them in the wild. Hands-on activities are also popular. Many resident and nonresident anglers enjoy pursuing Missouri's game fish. The sport offers a great chance to enjoy the outdoors with friends and family, and in many cases, bring home a healthy meal of fresh fish.

Proceeds from license sales, along with special taxes anglers pay on fishing supplies and motorboat fuel, fund the majority of fish management efforts, including fish surveys, the development of special regulations and stocking programs. The sport also has a huge impact on Missouri's economy, supporting thousands of jobs in fishing, tourism and related industries.

CATCH-AND-RELEASE FISHING

Selective harvest (keeping some fish to eat and releasing the rest) and total catch-and-release fishing allow anglers to enjoy the sport without harming the resource. Catch-and-release is especially important with overharvested species. Biologists are trying to improve these fisheries by protecting large adults of breeding age. The fishing regulations available at the Missouri Department of Conservation's website and your local fisheries' office are excellent sources of advice on which fish to keep and which to release.

Catch-and-release is only truly successful if the fish survives the experience. Here are some helpful tips to reduce the chances of post-release mortality.

- Play and land fish quickly.

- Wet your hands before touching a fish to avoid removing its protective slime coating.

- Handle the fish gently and keep it in the water as much as possible.

- Do not hold the fish by the eyes or gills. Hold it by the lower lip or under the gill plate—and support its belly.

- If a fish is deeply hooked, cut the line so at least an inch hangs outside the mouth. This helps the hook lie flush when the fish takes in food.

- Circle hooks may help reduce the number of deeply hooked fish.

- Avoid fishing in deep water unless you plan to keep your catch.

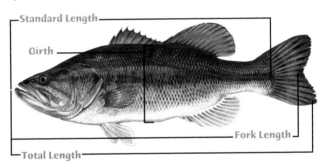

FISH MEASUREMENT

Fish are measured in three ways: standard length, fork length and total length. The first two are more accurate, because tails are often damaged or worn down. Total length is used in slot limits.

The following formulas estimate the weight of popular game fish. Lengths are in inches; weight is in pounds.

Formulas
 Bass weight = (length x length x girth) / 1,200
 Pike weight = (length x length x length) / 3,500

Sunfish weight = (length x length x length) / 1,200
Trout weight = (length x girth x girth) / 800
Walleye weight = (length x length x length) / 2,700

For example, let's say that you catch a 16-inch Walleye. Using the formula for Walleyes above: (16 x 16 x 16) divided by 2,700 = 1.5 pounds. Your Walleye would weigh approximately 1.5 pounds.

MISSOURI STATE RECORD FISH

The Missouri Department of Conservation maintains a list of record fish caught in Missouri as well as other fishing records at its website, http://mdc.mo.gov/fish/records

SPECIES	WEIGHT (LBS.-OZ.)	WHERE CAUGHT	YEAR
Bass, Hybrid Black	5-10	Table Rock Lake	2004
Bass, Largemouth	13-14	Bull Shoals Lake	1961
Bass, Smallmouth	7-7	Stockton Lake	1994
Bass, Spotted	7-8	Table Rock Lake	1966
Bass, Striped	60-9	Bull Shoals Lake	2011
Bass, White	5-6	Table Rock Lake	2002
Bass, Yellow	0-9	Sandy Slough	1995
Bluegill	3-0	Farm Pond	1963
Bowfin	19-0	Duck Creek	1963
Buffalo, Bigmouth	56-0	Loch-Loma Lake	1976
Buffalo, Black	53-0	Wappapello Lake	1989
Buffalo, Smallmouth	36-12	Lake of the Ozarks	1986
Bullhead, Black	4-11	Binder Lake	1977
Bullhead, Brown	3-3	Loch-Loma Lake	1990
Bullhead, Yellow	6-6	Old Drexel Lake	2006
Burbot	OPEN		
Carp, Bighead	80-0	Lake of the Ozarks	2004
Carp, Common	50-6	Rothwell Park Lake	1996
Carp, Grass	69-0	Crowder State Park	2002
Carpsucker, Highfin	OPEN		
Carpsucker, River	2-3	South Grand River	2008
Catfish, Blue	130-0	Missouri River	2010
Catfish, Channel	34-10	Lake Jacomo	1976
Catfish, Flathead	77-8	Montrose Lake	2003
Catfish, White	OPEN		
Crappie, Black	5-0	Private Pond	2006
Crappie, White	4-9	Farm Pond	2000
Drum	40-8	Lake of the Ozarks	1980
Eel, American	4-8	Meramec River	1993
Flier	0-10	Farm Pond	1991
Gar, Alligator (bow)	127-0	Diversion Channel	2007
Gar, Shortnose	8-3	Lake Contrary	2010
Gar, Longnose	27-0	Bull Shoals Lake	1999
Gar, Spotted	6-0	Boeuf Creek	2005
Goggle-eye	2-12	Big Piney River	1968
Goldeye	1-12	Lake of the Ozarks	2012
Herring, Skipjack	1-11	Osage River	2005
Mooneye	0-13	Meramec River	1999

SPECIES	WEIGHT (LBS.-OZ.)	WHERE CAUGHT	YEAR
Muskellunge	41-2	Lake of the Ozarks	1981
Muskellunge, Tiger	22-0	Stockton Lake	1986
Paddlefish	108-8	Lake Jacomo	1988
Perch, White	OPEN		
Perch, Yellow	1-11	Bull Shoals Lake	2009
Pickerel, Chain	5-1	Clearwater Spillway	1974
Pickerel, Grass	1-3	Farm Pond	2005
Pike, Northern	18-9	Stockton Lake	1975
Quillback	2-12	North Fabius River	2003
Redhorse, Black	1-8	Meramec River	1995
Redhorse, Golden	5-1	Niangua River	2004
Redhorse, River	9-10	Osage River	2006
Redhorse, Shorthead	2-14	Truman Lake	2009
Redhorse, Silver	5-10	Sac River	2000
Sauger	5-1	Osage River	1994
Shad, Gizzard	1-6	Truman Dam	2001
Striper, Hybrid	20-8	Osage River	1986
Sturgeon, Shovelnose	4-0	Des Moines River	2001
Sucker, Blue	9-14	Missouri River	1997
Sucker, Northern Hog	3-5	Current River	1988
Sucker, Spotted	OPEN		
Sucker, White	4-8	Lake Taneycomo	1990
Sunfish, Green	2-2	Stockton Lake	1971
Sunfish, Hybrid	2-3	Farm Pond	1997
Sunfish, Longear	0-11	Private Pond	2007
Sunfish, Redear	2-7	Wetstone Creek Cons. Area	1988
Sunfish, Red Spotted	0-2	Castor River	1991
Trout, Rainbow	18-1	Roaring River	2004
Trout, Brown	28-12	Lake Taneycomo	2009
Walleye	21-1	Bull Shoals Lake	1988
Warmouth	1-4	Farm Pond	1984

FISH CONSUMPTION ADVISORIES

Most fish are safe to eat, but pollutants are a valid concern. Missouri routinely monitors contaminant levels and issues advisories and recommendations about eating sport fish caught in the wild. Missouri Department of Health and Senior Services website. http://dhss.mo.gov

These pages explain how the information is presented for each fish.

SAMPLE FISH ILLUSTRATION

Description: brief summary of physical characteristics to help you identify the fish, such as coloration and markings, body shape, fin size and placement

Similar Species: lists other fish that look similar and the pages on which they can be found; also includes detailed inset drawings (below) highlighting physical traits such as markings, mouth size or shape and fin characteristics to help you distinguish this fish from similar species

Rainbow Trout	**Brown Trout**	**Rainbow Trout**	**Brown Trout**
reddish-pink longitudinal stripe	orange or reddish spots	forked tail, prominent dark spots	squared tail, spots faint or absent

SAMPLE COMPARE ILLUSTRATIONS

COMMON NAME
Scientific Name

Other Names: common terms or nicknames you may hear to describe this species

Habitat: environment where the fish is found (such as streams, rivers, small or large lakes, fast-flowing or still water, in or around vegetation, near shore, in clear water)

Range: geographic distribution, starting with the fish's overall range, followed by state-specific information

Food: what the fish eats most of the time (such as crustaceans, insects, fish, plankton)

Reproduction: timing of and behavior during the spawning period (dates and water temperatures, migration information, preferred spawning habitat, type of nest if applicable, colonial or solitary nester, parental care for eggs or fry)

Average Size: average length or range of length, average weight or range of weight

Records: State—the state record for this species, including location and year; North American—the North American record for this species, including location and year (based on the Fresh Water Fishing Hall of Fame)

Notes: Interesting natural history information. This can include unique behaviors, remarkable features, sporting and table quality, details on migrations, seasonal patterns or population trends.

Description: brownish-green back and sides with white belly; long, stout body; rounded tail; continuous dorsal fin; bony plates covering head; males have a large "eye" spot at the base of the tail

Similar Species: Burbot (pg. 42)

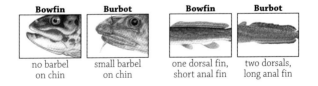

Bowfin	Burbot	Bowfin	Burbot
no barbel on chin	small barbel on chin	one dorsal fin, short anal fin	two dorsals, long anal fin

BOWFIN
Amia calva

Other Names: dogfish, grindle or grinnel, mudfish, cypress trout, lake lawyer, beaverfish

Habitat: deep waters associated with vegetation in warmwater lakes and rivers; feeds in shallow weedbeds

Range: Mississippi River drainage east through the St. Lawrence drainage, south from Texas to Florida; Missouri—backwaters of the Missouri and Mississippi Rivers and the lowlands of southeast Missouri

Food: fish, crayfish

Reproduction: in spring when water temperature exceeds 61 degrees, male removes vegetation to build a nest in sand or gravel; one or more females deposit up to 5,000 eggs in the nest; male guards the nest and the "ball" of young

Average Size: 12 to 24 inches, 2 to 5 pounds

Records: State—19 pounds, Duck Creek, 1993; North American—21 pounds, 8 ounces, Forest Lake, South Carolina, 1980

Notes: A voracious predator, the Bowfin prowls shallow weedbeds preying on anything that moves. Once thought detrimental to game fish populations, it is now considered an asset in controlling rough fish and stunted game fish. An air breather that tolerates low oxygen levels, Bowfins can survive buried in mud for short periods during drought conditions. Bowfins are common along the Mississippi River above the Missouri River mouth and in southeastern Missouri. They are considered inedible by most anglers.

25

Description: black to olive-green back; sides yellowish-green; belly creamy white to yellow; light bar at the base of the tail; barbels around mouth are dark at the base; adipose fin; lacks scales; round tail; anal fin 17–21 rays

Similar Species: Brown Bullhead (pg. 28), Yellow Bullhead (pg. 30), Flathead Catfish (pg. 36), Madtom/Stonecat (pg. 40)

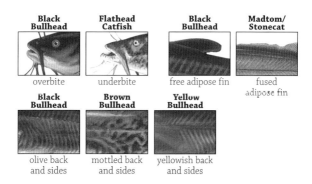

Black Bullhead	Flathead Catfish	Black Bullhead	Madtom/ Stonecat
overbite	underbite	free adipose fin	fused adipose fin

Black Bullhead	Brown Bullhead	Yellow Bullhead
olive back and sides	mottled back and sides	yellowish back and sides

BLACK BULLHEAD

Ameiurus melas

Other Names: common bullhead, horned pout

Habitat: shallow, slow-moving streams and backwaters; lakes and ponds—tolerates extremely turbid (cloudy) conditions

Range: Southern Canada through the Great Lakes and the Mississippi River watershed to the Southwest and into Mexico; Missouri—present statewide, common in northern prairie counties

Food: a scavenging opportunist; feeds mostly on animal material (dead or alive) but will eat plant matter

Reproduction: spawns from late April to early June; builds nest in shallow water with a muddy bottom; both sexes guard nest, eggs and young to 1 inch in size

Average Size: 8 to 10 inches, 4 ounces to 1 pound

Records: State—4 pounds, 11 ounces, Binder Lake, 1977; North American—8 pounds, 15 ounces, Sturgis Pond, Michigan, 1987

Notes: The Black Bullhead is the most widespread and common bullhead in Missouri, but it is most prevalent in the northern prairie streams. It is also the bullhead species most tolerant of silt, pollution and low oxygen levels. Bullheads tend to be nocturnal but can be caught throughout the day. As table fare, bullheads get little respect, but they are bigger than most panfish taken home to eat, and just as tasty.

Description: yellowish-brown upper body, with mottling on back and sides; barbels around mouth; adipose fin; lacks scales; rounded tail; well-defined barbs on the pectoral spines; anal fin 22–23 rays

Similar Species: Black Bullhead (pg. 26), Yellow Bullhead (pg. 30), Flathead Catfish (pg. 36), Madtom/Stonecat (pg. 40)

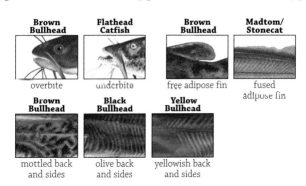

Brown Bullhead	Flathead Catfish	Brown Bullhead	Madtom/Stonecat
overbite	underbite	free adipose fin	fused adipose fin

Brown Bullhead	Black Bullhead	Yellow Bullhead
mottled back and sides	olive back and sides	yellowish back and sides

BROWN BULLHEAD

Ameiurus nebulosus

Other Names: marbled or speckled bullhead, red cat

Habitat: warm, weedy lakes and sluggish streams

Range: Southern Canada through the Great Lakes down the eastern states to Florida, introduced in the West; Missouri—Duck Creek Wildlife Area; a few stocked lakes

Food: scavenging opportunist feeding mostly on insects, fish, fish eggs, snails, some plant matter

Reproduction: in early summer male builds nest in shallow water with good vegetation and a sand or rocky bottom; both sexes guard the eggs and young

Average Size: 8 to 10 inches, 4 ounces to 2 pounds

Records: State—3 pounds, 3 ounces, Loch Loma, 1990; North American—6 pounds, 2 ounces, Pearl River, Mississippi, 1991

Notes: The Brown Bullhead is rare in Missouri with the only sustaining population in the Duck Creek Wildlife Refuge in southeastern Missouri. There are reportedly a few other populations around the state that are the results of accidental or intentional introductions. Adults are very involved in rearing their young, first by agitating the eggs then guarding the fry until they grow to about one inch long. The young are black and can often be seen swimming in a tight, swarming ball. Like other catfish, bullheads are primarily nocturnal feeders. Brown Bullhead have red flesh with good flavor and texture.

29

Description: dark-olive head and back; yellowish-green sides; white belly; barbels on lower jaw are pale green or white; adipose fin; lacks scales; rounded tail; anal fin 24–27 rays

Similar Species: Black Bullhead (pg. 26), Brown Bullhead (pg. 28), Flathead Catfish (pg. 36), Madtom/Stonecat (pg. 40)

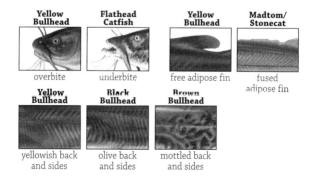

Yellow Bullhead	Flathead Catfish	Yellow Bullhead	Madtom/ Stonecat
overbite	underbite	free adipose fin	fused adipose fin

Yellow Bullhead	Black Bullhead	Brown Bullhead
yellowish back and sides	olive back and sides	mottled back and sides

YELLOW BULLHEAD

Ameiurus natalis

Other Names: white-whiskered bullhead, yellow cat

Habitat: well-vegetated, warm lakes and sluggish streams

Range: southern Great Lakes through the eastern half of the US to the Gulf and into Mexico, introduced in the West; Missouri—common throughout the state

Food: scavenging opportunist, feeds on insects, crayfish, snails, small fish and plant material

Reproduction: in late spring to early summer, males build a nest in shallow water with some vegetation and a soft bottom; both sexes guard the eggs and young

Average Size: 8 to 10 inches, 1 to 2 pounds

Records: State—6 pounds, 6 ounces, Old Drexel Lake, 2006; North American—4 pounds, 15 ounces, Ogeechee River, Georgia, 2003 (not recorded as a North American record)

Notes: The Yellow Bullhead is the bullhead species least tolerant of turbidity and prefers low-gradient streams, but it will occupy ponds if they are reasonably clear. Bullheads feed by "taste," locating food by following chemical trails through the water. This ability can be greatly diminished in polluted water, impairing their ability to find food. The Yellow Bullhead is less likely than other bullhead species to overpopulate a lake and become stunted.

Description: pale blue back and sides, large fish may be dark bluish-gray; no spots; forked tail; anal fin straight on rear edge with 30–35 rays; adipose fin; long barbels around mouth

Similar Species: Channel Catfish (pg. 34), White Catfish (pg. 38)

Blue Catfish	Channel Catfish	White Catfish
30 to 36 rays in anal fin, no spots, straight-edged anal fin	24 to 29 rays in anal fin, spots, curved anal fin	19 to 23 rays in anal fin, no spots, curved anal fin

BLUE CATFISH

Ictalurus furcatus

Other Names: white, silver, Mississippi or river cat

Habitat: swift current or deep-lowing pools of large rivers; large impoundments; stocked in smaller impoundments for specialized fishing

Range: the Mississippi and Ohio River drainages in central US, introduced in the West; Missouri—common in the Missouri, Osage and Mississippi Rivers and mouths of their larger tributary streams

Food: small fish, often dead or injured shad

Reproduction: adults mature at 4 to 6 years; spawning occurs in sheltered areas at the edge of currents, often in cavities or behind rocks; eggs and fry are guarded by adults

Average Size: 2 to 3 feet, 20 to 40 pounds

Records: State—103 pounds, Missouri River, 1991; North American—121 pounds, 8 ounces, Lake Texoma, Texas, 2004

Notes: The Blue Catfish is the largest US catfish. They occupy the fast water of large rivers and were widespread in the central states before these rivers were dammed. There are stable Missouri populations in the Missouri and Osage Rivers and below the mouth of the Missouri River in the Mississippi. Blue Catfish are big-water fish that prefer deep pools with a swift current. They often suspend below large schools of shad. Like other catfish, Blue Catfish have firm, white flesh with good flavor.

Description: steel-gray to silver back and sides; white belly; young fish have black spots on the sides; large fish lack spots and appear dark olive or slate; forked tail; adipose fin; long barbels around mouth

Similar Species: Bullheads (pp. 26–30), Blue Catfish (pg. 32), White Catfish (pg. 38)

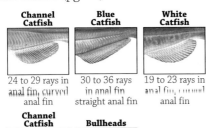

Channel Catfish	Blue Catfish	White Catfish
24 to 29 rays in anal fin, curved anal fin	30 to 36 rays in anal fin straight anal fin	19 to 23 rays in anal fin, curved anal fin

Channel Catfish	Bullheads
deeply forked tail	tail rounded or slightly notched

CHANNEL CATFISH

Ictalurus punctatus

Other Names: spotted, speckled or silver catfish

Habitat: prefers clean, fast-moving streams with deep pools; stocked in many lakes; can tolerate turbid waters

Range: southern Canada through the Midwest to the Gulf of Mexico into Mexico and Florida; introduced throughout much of the United States; Missouri—common throughout the state

Food: insects, crustaceans, fish, some plant debris

Reproduction: in early summer, male builds a nest in a dark, sheltered area such as an undercut bank or log; female deposits gelatinous eggs; male guards the eggs and young until the nest is deserted

Average Size: 12 to 20 inches, 3 to 4 pounds

Records: State—34 pounds, 10 ounces, Lake Jacomo, 1976; North American—58 pounds, Santee Cooper Reservoir, South Carolina, 1964

Notes: This highly respected sport fish is one of the most popular fish in the state and Missouri's state fish. It is abundant in lakes and reservoirs and often stocked in ponds but prefers clear, moving water. Like other catfish, Channel Catfish are nocturnal and are most successfully fished for at night. Channels put up a strong fight and are fine table fare. They were the first widely farmed fish in the US and are now common in grocery stores and restaurants throughout the country.

35

Description: color variable, usually mottled yellow or brown; belly cream to yellow; adipose fin; chin barbels; lacks scales; tail squared; head broad and flattened; pronounced underbite

Similar Species: Bullheads (pp. 26–30), Channel Catfish (pg. 34), White Catfish (pg. 38)

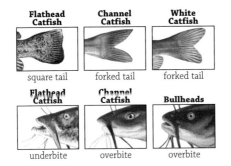

Flathead Catfish	Channel Catfish	White Catfish
square tail	forked tail	forked tail

Flathead Catfish	Channel Catfish	Bullheads
underbite	overbite	overbite

FLATHEAD CATFISH
Pylodictis olivaris

Other Names: shovelnose, shovelhead; yellow, mud, pied or Mississippi cat

Habitat: deep pools of large rivers and impoundments

Range: the Mississippi River watershed and into Mexico; large rivers in the Southwest; Missouri—common in rivers and impoundments throughout most of the state; uncommon in Ozark streams

Food: fish, crayfish

Reproduction: spawns when water is 72 to 80 degrees; male builds and defends nest, which is in a hollow log, an undercut bank or another sheltered area; large females may lay up to 30,000 eggs

Average Size: 20 to 30 inches, 10 to 20 pounds

Records: State—77 pounds, 8 ounces, Montrose Lake, 2003; North American—123 pounds, Elk River Reservoir, Kansas, 1998

Notes: The Flathead Catfish is a solitary predator that feeds aggressively on live fish, often at night. It is frequently found near logjams or in deep pools at night, and it hides in bank holes during the day. A tenacious fighter, it is known for its firm, white flesh. Flatheads have been introduced into a few lakes in an attempt to control stunted panfish populations with generally poor results. Flatheads are common throughout Missouri except in the clear, fast Ozark streams.

Description: bluish-silver body and off-white belly; older fish are dark blue with some mottling; forked tail with rounded lobes; lacks scales; adipose fin; white chin barbels

Similar Species: Bullheads (pp. 26–30), Channel Catfish (pg. 34)

White Catfish

moderately forked tail, rounded lobes

Channel Catfish

deeply forked tail, pointed lobes

Bullheads

rounded tail

White Catfish

19 to 23 rays in anal fin

Channel Catfish

24 to 30 rays in anal fin

WHITE CATFISH

Ictaluridae

Ameiurus catus

Other Names: whitey, silver or weed catfish

Habitat: freshwater and slightly brackish water in coastal streams and lakes

Range: Maine south to Florida and west to Texas; introduced in some western states; Missouri-fee-fishing lakes with occasional escapees in streams and reservoirs

Food: insects, crayfish, small fish and plant debris

Reproduction: male builds nest in sheltered area with a sand or gravel bottom when water temperatures reach the high 60s; both sexes guard nest and eggs until fry disperse

Average Size: 10 to 18 inches, 1 to 2 pounds

Records: State (bank line)—7 pounds, 4 ounces, Truman Lake, 1991; North American—22 pounds, William Land Park Pond, California, 1994

Notes: The White Catfish is not native to Missouri but was introduced in order to stock fee-fishing lakes. In terms of habits, White Catfish prefer quieter water than Channel Catfish with a somewhat firmer bottom than that sought by bullheads. They frequent the edge of weedbeds and are often caught when still-fishing the bottom near deep water. White Catfish are not considered a prized sport fish, but they have firm flesh and fine flavor.

STONECAT

SLENDER MADTOM

Description: Slender Madtom—dark olive to brown; dark outline on fins and squared tail; large, fleshy head; Stonecat —dark brown; rounded tail; protruding upper jaw; both species have an adipose fin that is continuous with tail

Similar Species: Bullheads (pp. 26–30), Catfish (pp. 34–38)

Stonecat	Slender Madtom
no dark outline on fins	dark outline on tail, anal and dorsal fins

Stonecat	Slender Madtom	Bullheads	Catfish
fused adipose fin	fused adipose fin	free adipose fin	free adipose fin

STONECAT *Noturus flavus*
SLENDER MADTOM *Noturus exilis*

Other Names: willow cat

Habitat: vegetated water near shore in medium to large lakes, under rocks in stream riffles

Range: Both—the eastern US; Missouri—Slender Madtom are common except in northwest; Stonecat prevalent in the northern two thirds of state

Food: small invertebrates, algae and other plant matter

Reproduction: spawns in late spring; female lays eggs under objects such as roots, rocks, logs or in abandoned crayfish burrows; eggs guarded by one parent

Average Size: Slender Madtom—3 to 5 inches; Stonecat—4 to 6 inches

Records: none

Notes: Madtoms are small, secretive fish that are most active at night. Both species have poison glands under the skin at the base of the dorsal and pectoral fins. Though not lethal, the poison produces a painful burning sensation, reputed to bring even the hardiest anglers to their knees, if only for a short time. Stonecats, and to a lesser extent, madtoms, are a common baitfish in some areas. Reportedly, damaging the "slime" coating (by rolling them in sand) to make handling easier will reduce their effectiveness as bait.

Description: mottled brown with a creamy chin and belly; eel-like body; small barbel at each nostril opening; longer barbel on chin; long dorsal fin that is similar to (and just above) anal fin

Similar Species: Bowfin (pg. 24)

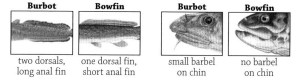

Burbot	Bowfin	Burbot	Bowfin
two dorsals, long anal fin	one dorsal fin, short anal fin	small barbel on chin	no barbel on chin

BURBOT
Lota lota

Gadidae

Other Names: lawyer, eelpout, ling, cusk

Habitat: deep, cold, clear, rock-bottomed lakes and streams

Range: northern North America into Siberia and across northern Europe; Missouri—rare in the Missouri and Mississippi Rivers; stocked in a few fee-fishing lakes

Food: primarily small fish, but renowned for attempting to eat almost anything, including fish eggs, clams and crayfish

Reproduction: pairs to large groups spawn together in mid- to-late winter under the ice over a sand or gravel bottom in less than 15 feet of water; after spawning, thrashing adults scatter fertilized eggs; no nest is built and there is no parental care

Average Size: 20 inches, 2 to 8 pounds

Records: State—open; North American—22 pounds, 8 ounces, Little Athapapuskow Lake, Manitoba, 1994

Notes: The Burbot is a coldwater fish, seldom found in fisheries where the water temperature routinely exceeds 69 degrees. It is popular with ice fishermen in North Dakota, eastern Wyoming and Scandinavia and considered a nuisance in other regions. Burbots are rare in Missouri but are occasionally caught in the Mississippi and Missouri Rivers. They have been stocked in a few commercial fishing lakes near St. Louis.

Description: gray back with purple or bronze reflections; silver sides; white underbelly; humped back; dorsal fin extends from hump to near tail; lateral line runs from head through the tail

Similar Species: White Bass (pg. 182)

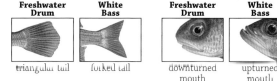

Freshwater Drum	White Bass	Freshwater Drum	White Bass
triangular tail	forked tail	downturned mouth	upturned mouth

FRESHWATER DRUM

Aplodinotus grunniens

Other Names: sheepshead, croaker, thunderpumper, grinder, bubbler, (commercially marketed as white perch)

Habitat: slow-to moderate current areas of rivers and streams; shallow lakes with soft bottoms; prefers turbid water

Range: Canada south through the Midwest into eastern Mexico to Guatemala; Missouri—common throughout the state

Food: small fish, insects, crayfish, clams

Reproduction: in May and June after water temperatures reach about 66 degrees, schools of drum lay eggs near the surface in open water over sand or gravel; no parental care of fry

Average Size: 10 to 14 inches, 2 to 5 pounds

Records: State—40 pounds, 8 ounces, Lake of the Ozarks, 1980; North American—54 pounds, 8 ounces, Nickajack Lake, Tennessee, 1972

Notes: The only freshwater member of a large family of marine fish, Drums are named for a grunting noise that is made by males, primarily to attract females. The sound is produced when specialized muscles rub along the swim bladder. The skull contains two enlarged L-shaped earstones called otoliths, once prized for jewelry by Native Americans. The flesh is flaky, white and tasty but easily dries out when cooked, due to its low oil content.

Description: dark brown on top with yellow sides and a white belly; long, snake-like body with a large mouth, pectoral fins and gill slits; a continuous dorsal, tail and anal fin

Similar Species: Native Lampreys (pg. 66)

American Eel

one gill cover, pectoral fins

Native Lampreys

seven gill slits, no pectoral fins

AMERICAN EEL

Anguilla rostrata

Other Names: common, Boston, Atlantic or freshwater eel

Habitat: soft bottoms of medium to large streams; brackish tidewater areas

Range: the Atlantic Ocean; eastern and central North America and eastern Central America; Missouri—rare in larger streams in eastern Missouri

Food: insects, crayfish, small fish

Reproduction: a "catadromous" species, it spends most of its life in freshwater, returning to the Sargasso Sea in the North Atlantic Ocean to spawn; females lay up to 20 million eggs; adults die after spawning

Average Size: 24 to 36 inches, 1 to 3 pounds

Records: State—4 pounds, 8 ounces, Meramec River, 1993; North American—8 pounds, 8 ounces, Cliff Pond, Massachusetts, 1992

Notes: Leaf-shaped larval eels drift with ocean currents for about a year after hatching in the Sargasso Sea. When they reach river mouths of North and Central America, they morph into small eels (elvers). Males remain in the estuaries; females migrate upstream. At maturity (up to 20 years of age) adults return to the Sargasso Sea. Before settlement, eels commonly migrated up the Mississippi River to Missouri; with the many dams now in place, few eels reach this far inland.

Description: olive to brown body mottled toward the head, but spotted at the rear and on rear fins; long, cylindrical profile; single dorsal fin located just above the anal fin; body encased in hard, plate-like scales; broad snout; two rows of large teeth on each side of upper jaw

Similar Species: Shortnose Gar (pg. 52), Longnose Gar (pg. 50), Spotted Gar (pg. 54)

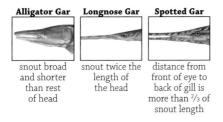

Alligator Gar	**Longnose Gar**	**Spotted Gar**
snout broad and shorter than rest of head	snout twice the length of the head	distance from front of eye to back of gill is more than ⅔ of snout length

ALLIGATOR GAR

Atractosteus spatula

Other Names: garfish, spotted gar, kingfish

Habitat: backwaters of large rivers

Range: northeastern Mexico, north up the Mississippi basin to the Missouri and the lower Ohio Rivers; Missouri— Mississippi River

Food: fish

Reproduction: adhesive eggs are deposited in weedy shallows when water temperatures reach the high 60s; no parental care

Average Size: 36 to 48 inches, 30 to 60 pounds

Records: State (bow)—127 pounds, Diversion Channel, 2007; North American—279 pounds, Rio Grande River, 1951

Notes: The Alligator Gar is one of the most spectacular fish in North America, reaching 8 feet in length and nearly 300 pounds. Like other gar, their hard mouth and sharp teeth make them difficult to hook and land. Over most of their range they are now quite rare, but a reasonable population still exists in Florida and Texas. Alligator Gar are rare in Missouri and are only likely to be encountered in the Mississippi River. Alligator Gar prefer deep backwater pools in large rivers, but may enter the mouths of tributary streams.

Description: olive to brown with dark spots along sides; long, cylindrical profile; single dorsal fin located just above the anal fin; body is encased in hard, plate-like scales; snout twice as long as head; needle-sharp teeth on both jaws

Similar Species: Shortnose Gar (pg. 52), Spotted Gar (pg. 54)

Longnose Gar	**Shortnose Gar**	**Spotted Gar**
snout length is 15 to 20 times its width; no spots on top of head or snout	snout length is 5 to 6 times its width	spots on head and snout

LONGNOSE GAR

Lepisosteus osseus

Other Names: garfish

Habitat: quiet waters of larger rivers and lakes

Range: central US throughout the Mississippi drainage south into Mexico, a few rivers in the northeast in the Great Lakes drainage; Missouri—common statewide

Food: minnows and other small fish

Reproduction: lays large, green eggs in weedy shallows when water temperatures reach the high 60s; using a small disk on the snout, a newly-hatched gar attaches to nearby plants, rocks, or branches until its digestive tract develops enough to begin feeding

Average Size: 1 to 3 feet, 2 to 5 pounds

Records: State—27 pounds, Bull Shoals Lake, 1999; North American—50 pounds, 5 ounces, Trinity River, Texas, 1954

Notes: The Longnose Gar belongs to a prehistoric family of fish that can breathe air with the aid of a modified swim bladder. This adaptation makes them well suited to survive in increasingly polluted rivers and lakes. They hunt by floating motionless near the surface then make a swift, sideways slash to capture prey. Gar are a valuable asset in controlling the increasing populations of rough fish. Longnose Gar are common statewide and the only gar species found in the clear, fast Ozark streams. Gar are not often fished for but are often the target of bow fishermen.

Description: head, back and sides are olive to slate-green; long, cylindrical body; single dorsal fin located just above the anal fin; body encased in hard, plate-like scales; snout a third longer than its head; needle-sharp teeth on both jaws

Similar Species: Longnose Gar (pg. 50), Spotted Gar (pg. 54)

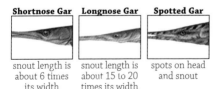

Shortnose Gar	**Longnose Gar**	**Spotted Gar**
snout length is about 6 times its width	snout length is about 15 to 20 times its width	spots on head and snout

SHORTNOSE GAR

Lepisosteus platostomas

Other Names: stubnose, broadnose or shortbilled gar

Habitat: open water of warm, slow-moving streams, backwaters and shallow oxbow lakes

Range: the Mississippi River drainage from the southern Great Lakes to Mexico; Missouri—common statewide except in the Ozarks, where it is rare

Food: minnows and small fish, crayfish

Reproduction: spawns in weedy backwaters when water temperatures reach the mid-60s; the large, yellowish-green eggs are poisonous to mammals

Average Size: 1 to 2 feet, 1 to 3 pounds

Records: State—4 pounds, 11 ounces, Lower Big Lake, 1995; North American—50 pounds, 5 ounces, Trinity River, Texas, 1954

Notes: The Shortnose Gar is smaller and not as widespread in Missouri as the Longnose Gar. Shortnose Gar are mostly absent from the Ozark streams. They prefer somewhat more active water and can tolerate more turbidity than other gar species. Like other gar species, it can "gulp" air and can withstand very warm and poorly oxygenated water. It is an ambush hunter and is frequently seen floating near brush piles at the current's edge. It has a strong, fishy flavor and is not often sought by anglers, but is the frequent target of bowfishermen.

Description: olive back and sides; spots on entire body including snout, fins, and tail; cylindrical body; narrow snout slightly longer than the head; sharp teeth on both jaws

Similar Species: Longnose Gar (pg. 50), Shortnose Gar (pg. 52)

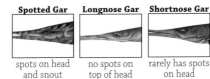

Spotted Gar	Longnose Gar	Shortnose Gar
spots on head and snout	no spots on top of head or snout	rarely has spots on head and snout

SPOTTED GAR

Lepisosteus oculatus

Other Names: speckled gar

Habitat: quiet, clear, weedy water in streams and lakes

Range: southern Great Lakes Basin southeast to Florida; Missouri—common in lowlands of southeastern Missouri

Food: minnows, small fish and insects

Reproduction: spawns in weedy backwaters when water temperatures reach the mid-60s; adhesive eggs are scattered over vegetation, algae mats or standing timber; no parental care

Average Size: 1 to 2 feet, 1 to 2 pounds

Records: State—6 pounds, Boeuf Creek, 2005; North American—28 pounds, 8 ounces, Lake Seminole, Florida, 1987

Notes: The Spotted Gar is the smallest gar in Missouri, and the species that requires the clearest water and the most vegetation. With increased runoff, many streams are becoming too turbid for this small gar. Like other gars, it can breathe air with the help of a modified swim bladder; it can therefore tolerate very warm, poorly oxygenated water. The Spotted Gar is a fun aquarium fish and is often sold in pet shops, but it requires live food to do well.

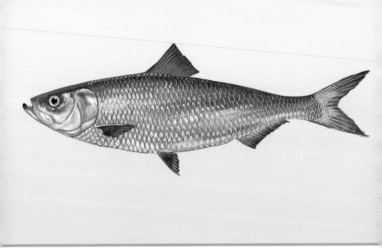

Description: deep, laterally compressed silver body with a blue-green back; no dark spots on shoulder; sharply pointed scales along belly (scutes)

Similar Species: Alabama Shad (pg. 58), Gizzard Shad (pg. 60)

Skipjack Herring	**Alabama Shad**	**Gizzard Shad**
underbite, speckles on tip of lower jaw	jaw even with snout, speckles on length of lower jaw	snout protruding over mouth

Skipjack Herring	**Gizzard Shad**
no long thread on last ray of dorsal fin	long thread on last dorsal ray

SKIPJACK HERRING

Alosa chrysochloris

Other Names: river herring, skipper

Habitat: clear water in large rivers, often at the mouth of tributary streams and below dams

Range: Gulf Coast waters from Texas to Florida, the Mississippi River, its large tributaries and impoundments; Missouri—common in Mississippi River below the Ohio River, rare in large tributary streams

Food: small fish, insects

Reproduction: little is known about its spawning habits, but individuals or small schools seem to spawn in clear water in early spring near the mouth of tributary streams

Average Size: 12 to 16 inches, 1 to 2 pounds

Records: State—1 pound, 11 ounces, Osage River, 2005; North American—3 pounds, 12 ounces, White Bear Lake, Tennessee, 1982

Notes: The Skipjack Herring is a very fast fish that gets its name from the spectacular leaps out of the water it makes as it chases prey. Skipjacks are fish of the big rivers, and don't often enter smaller tributaries. Skipjacks are most common below the Mississippi River dams but they may be encountered in any large tributary stream. They feed on the surface and prefer the clear, less turbid parts of the river. Skipjacks readily take flies and small lures, and on light tackle it is one of Missouri's most exciting fish, as it fights hard and makes spectacular leaps.

57

Description: silver body and blue-gray back; one dark spot on the shoulder; mouth is large and extends to the back of the eye; dark spots on lower jaw; saw-tooth edge formed by sharply pointed scales along the belly (scutes); upper and lower jaw are the same length

Similar Species: Gizzard Shad (pg. 60), Skipjack Herring (pg. 56)

Alabama Shad   **Gizzard Shad**   **Skipjack Herring**

jaw even with snout, speckles run the length of the lower jaw   snout protruding over mouth   underbite, speckles on tip of lower jaw

ALABAMA SHAD

Alosa alabamae

Other Names: river herring, silver or 'bama shad

Habitat: coastal marine areas for most of the year; migrates up large rivers to spawn; introduced in a few reservoirs

Range: the northern Gulf from Florida to Mississippi north through the Mississippi basin to the lower Ohio drainage; Missouri—the Mississippi and Missouri Rivers and a few large tributaries

Food: plankton feeders

Reproduction: migrates up spawning rivers when water temperatures reach 62 to 67 degrees; spawning takes place at night when eggs are released in moderate current over sand or gravel

Average Size: 10 to 18 inches, 8 ounces to 1 pound, 8 ounces

Records: none

Notes: The Alabama Shad are marine fish that enter large rivers to spawn, sometimes traveling hundreds of miles upstream. They were once abundant enough to be commercially harvested, but increased river turbidity and dam construction have greatly reduced the Alabama Shad population over most of its range. The only large remaining population spawns in the Apalachicola River in the Florida Panhandle but most years some still make it as far north as Missouri.

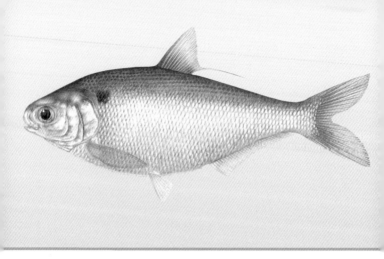

Description: deep, laterally compressed body; silvery-blue back with white sides and belly; young fish have a dark spot on shoulder behind the gill; small mouth; last rays of dorsal fin form a long thread

Similar Species: Skipjack Herring (pg. 56), Threadfin Shad (pg. 62)

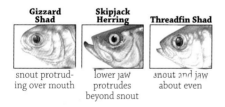

Gizzard Shad	Skipjack Herring	Threadfin Shad
snout protruding over mouth	lower jaw protrudes beyond snout	snout and jaw about even

GIZZARD SHAD
Dorosoma cepedianum

Other Names: hickory, mud or jack shad

Habitat: large rivers, reservoirs, lakes, swamps and temporarily flooded pools; brackish and saline waters in coastal areas

Range: St. Lawrence and Great Lakes, Mississippi, Atlantic and Gulf Slope drainages from Quebec to Mexico, south to central Florida; Missouri—common throughout the state

Food: herbivorous filter feeder

Reproduction: spawning takes place in tributary streams and along the lakeshore in early summer; schooling adults release eggs in open water without regard for individual mates

Average Size: 6 to 8 inches, 1 to 8 ounces

Records: State—1 pound, 6 ounces, Truman Dam, 2001; North American—4 pounds, 12 ounces, Lake Oahe, South Dakota, 2006

Notes: The Gizzard Shad is a widespread, prolific fish that is best known as forage for popular game fish. At times gizzard shad can become overabundant and experience large die-offs. The name "gizzard" refers to this shad's long, convoluted intestine that is often packed with sand. Though gizzard shad are a management problem at times, they form a valuable link in turning plankton into usable forage for large game fish. Occasionally larger Gizzard Shad are caught with hook and line, but they have little food value.

Description: silvery-yellow back with white sides and belly; dark spot on shoulder behind gill; deep laterally compressed body; small terminal mouth; last rays of dorsal fin form a long thread

Similar Species: Alabama Shad (pg. 58), Gizzard Shad (pg. 60)

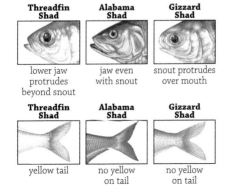

Threadfin Shad	**Alabama Shad**	**Gizzard Shad**
lower jaw protrudes beyond snout	jaw even with snout	snout protrudes over mouth
Threadfin Shad	**Alabama Shad**	**Gizzard Shad**
yellow tail	no yellow on tail	no yellow on tail

THREADFIN SHAD

Dorosoma petenense

Other Names: silver, yellow or thread shad

Habitat: current of large, warm rivers and reservoirs; brackish and saline waters in coastal areas

Range: southern Mississippi River drainage through the Gulf states south into Central America; Missouri—Mississippi River, occasionally stocked in reservoirs

Food: herbivorous filter feeder

Reproduction: schools of shad spawn in the shallows along the shore when water temperature reaches the low 70s, adhesive eggs are spread over vegetation and left unguarded

Average Size: 2 to 5 inches

Records: none

Notes: The Threadfin Shad is similar to the Gizzard Shad but it is smaller and prefers currents in rivers, or open water in reservoirs. It is a southern species that has spread into the central US since the 1950s. It requires warm water and dies when water temperatures drop below 41 degrees. When the water warms in summer, they migrate upstream and can become very abundant in the lower Mississippi below the mouth of the Ohio River.

Description: yellow-brown back; silver-blue sides; short gold stripe in front of dorsal fin; females and young have rows of brown spots on sides; reddish-brown in males; breeding males have bright blue sides with rows of red spots

Similar Species: Mosquitofish (pg. 68), Brook Silverside (pg. 114)

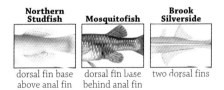

Northern Studfish	**Mosquitofish**	**Brook Silverside**
dorsal fin base above anal fin	dorsal fin base behind anal fin	two dorsal fins

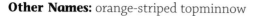
NORTHERN STUDFISH

Fundulus catenatus

Other Names: orange-striped topminnow

Habitat: clear, calm water at the edge of small to medium-sized streams with a hard bottom

Range: western Appalachian States west through Missouri Kansas and Oklahoma; Missouri—Ozark Region

Food: insects, small crustaceans

Reproduction: spawns over shallow gravel in late spring through summer; males establish territory along stream edges; male aggressively defends territory; eggs sink to the bottom and are left without parental care

Average Size: 2 to 6 inches

Records: none

Notes: The Northern Studfish is a very common and abundant fish in the clear streams of the Missouri Ozarks. Small schools of studfish patrol the shallow stream edges, often in water just a few inches deep. Northern Studfish avoid predators and nets by making quick jumps or flips that land them a foot or more from their starting point. Juveniles and female studfish are rather dull, but breeding males have spectacular, iridescent sides with rows of bright orange dots. Northern Studfish are too "jumpy" and aggressive in a tank or pail to make good aquarium or baitfish.

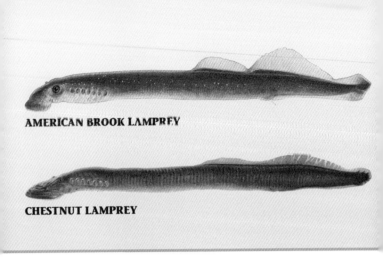

AMERICAN BROOK LAMPREY

CHESTNUT LAMPREY

Description: eel-like body; round, sucking-disk mouth; seven
paired gill openings; dorsal fin long, extending to tail; no
paired fins

Similar Species: American Eel (pg. 46)

Lampreys	American Eel
seven gill openings	one gill opening

NATIVE LAMPREYS

Ichthyomyzon, Lampetra

Petromyzontidae

Other Names: Chesnut and Silver Lamprey, American, Least, Southern, and Northern Brook Lampreys

Habitat: juveniles live in the quiet pools of streams and rivers; adults may move into some lakes

Range: the Mississippi and Ohio River drainages in the central US; Missouri—Chestnut Lamprey—common in lower Mississippi, less common in Ozarks and rest of state; Northern Brook Lamprey—most common lamprey in northern Ozark streams

Food: juvenile lampreys are bottom-dwellers and filter feeders in streams; adults are either parasitic on fish or do not feed

Reproduction: adults build nests in the gravel of streambeds when water temperatures reach the mid-50s then die soon after spawning

Average Size: 6 to 12 inches

Records: none

Notes: Lampreys are some of earth's oldest vertebrates, with fossil records dating back 500 million years. In Missouri, there are six native lampreys. The Chestnut and Silver Lampreys are parasitic in adult form, often leaving small, round wounds on their prey. The Brook Lampreys are non-parasitic. All of the native lampreys coexist with the other Missouri fish species with little or no effect on their populations. Due to deteriorating water conditions, many native lampreys are endangered or threatened throughout their range.

Description: olive-green back and sides; scales outlined giving sides cross-hatched appearance; upturned mouth; dark bar under eye; rounded tail fin; anal fin in males is long and pointed

Similar Species: Northern Studfish (pg. 64)

Mosquitofish

Northern Studfish

dorsal fin starts behind anal fin

dorsal fin starts forward of anal fin

MOSQUITOFISH
Gambusia affinis

Other Names: mosquito or surface minnow

Habitat: surface of shallow, well-vegetated backwaters with little current

Range: the southeastern US, introduced worldwide; Missouri—common throughout the state

Food: insects, crustaceans and some plant material

Reproduction: gives birth to live young after internal fertilization; may produce several broods in a single season

Average Size: 2 to 3 inches

Records: none

Notes: There are few native livebearers in the US, but it is a well-represented family in the tropical and subtropical Americas. The male Mosquitofish uses his modified anal fin to transfer sperm to the much larger female. Females can store sperm up to ten months and then give birth to live fry. Mosquitofish have been introduced worldwide to control mosquitoes but seem to be no better at pest control than native species. Mosquitofish have broad ecological tolerance and can survive high temperature, salinity and low oxygen levels.

Description: dark-gray to black back; silver-gray sides with dark blotches; low-set eyes; upturned mouth; tiny body scales, none on head

Similar Species: Common Carp (pg. 72), Grass Carp (pg. 76), Silver Carp (pg. 78)

Bighead Carp

small silver scales

Common Carp

large, yellow scales with a dark margin

Grass Carp

large, silver scales with a dark margin

Silver Carp

small silver scales

Bighead Carp

keeled belly from pelvic fin to anal fin

Silver Carp

keeled belly from gills to anal fin

Bighead/Silver Carp

eyes low on head

Common Carp

eyes high on head

BIGHEAD CARP

Hypophthalmichthys nobilis

Other Names: river carp, lake fish, speckled amur

Habitat: large, warm rivers and connected lakes

Range: Asia, introduced in other parts of the world; Missouri—the Mississippi and Missouri Rivers and a few large tributaries and impoundments

Food: aquatic vegetation and floating plankton, mostly algae

Reproduction: spawns from late spring to early summer in warm, flowing water

Average Size: 24 to 36 inches, 5 to 50 pounds

Records: State—80 pounds, Lake of the Ozarks, 2004; North American—90 pounds, Kirby Lake, Texas, 2000

Notes: Bighead Carp are the fourth most important aquaculture fish in the world. They were introduced to the US to control algae in southern aquaculture ponds and are now commonly farmed as a dual crop with catfish. They escaped to the Mississippi River and are now well established in the Ohio River and are the predominant fish in some areas. The Silver Carp, and to a lesser degree the Bighead Carp, makes high leaps from the water when frightened by boats. As filter feeders, Bighead Carp are targets for bowfishermen, but not anglers. They have a pleasant, mild flavor, but are bony and are not highly regarded table fare in this country.

Description: brassy yellow to dark-olive back and sides; whitish-yellow belly; round mouth has two pairs of barbels; reddish tail and anal fin; each scale has a dark margin

Similar Species: Bighead Carp (pg. 70), Grass Carp (pg. 76), Silver Carp (pg. 78)

Common Carp

large yellow scales with dark margin

Bighead/Silver Carp

small silver scales

Grass Carp

large silver scales with dark margin

Common Carp

eyes high on head

Bighead/Silver Carp

eyes low on head

COMMON CARP

Cyprinus carpio

Cyprinidae

Other Names: German, European, mirror or leather carp, buglemouth

Habitat: warm, shallow, quiet, well-vegetated waters of streams and lakes

Range: native to Asia, introduced throughout the world; Missouri—common statewide

Food: opportunistic feeder; prefers insect larvae, crustaceans and mollusks, but at times eats algae and some higher plants

Reproduction: spawns from late spring to early summer in very shallow water at stream and lake edges; very obvious when spawning, with a great deal of splashing

Average Size: 16 to 18 inches, 5 to 20 pounds

Records: State—50 pounds, 6 ounces, Rothwell Park Lake, 1993; North American—57 pounds, 13 ounces, Tidal Basin, Washington D.C., 1983

Notes: The carp is one of the world's most important freshwater fish. This fast-growing fish provides sport and food for millions of people throughout its range. This Asian minnow was introduced into Europe in the twelfth century, and into North America in the 1800s. Carp are a highly prized sport fish in Europe, but they have not gained the same status in the US. There is a significant commercial fishery for carp in both the Mississippi and the Missouri Rivers. Leather and Mirror Carp are Common Carp covered with skin and only few large scales.

FERAL GOLDFISH

RELEASED GOLDFISH

Description: body color is variable, goldfish can be
olive-green, red, orange, gold, pink, or variegated black
and orange; deep body, fins are heavy and rounded,
dorsal fin originates just above or behind pelvic fins

Similar Species: Common Carp (pg. 72)

Goldfish	Common Carp	Goldfish	Common Carp
no chin barbels	chin barbels	dorsal fin originates just above or behind pelvic fins	dorsal fin originates just ahead of pelvic fins

GOLDFISH

Carassius auratus

Other Names: Golden Carp, Indiana, Baltimore or Missouri minnow

Habitat: quiet well-vegetated stream pools, weedy lake edges

Range: native to Asia, introduced throughout the world; the central US from coast to coast; Missouri—not well established but often present statewide

Food: scavengers on both plant and animal matter

Reproduction: long spawning season from late spring through summer; spawns in very shallow water at stream and lake edges; very sticky eggs are spread over vegetation; no parental care

Average Size: 3 to 10 inches

Records: State—none; North American—3 pounds, 2 ounces, Lourdes Pond, Indiana, 2002

Notes: Goldfish are one of the most common baitfish in Missouri and many escape or are released annually, and pet goldfish are released as well. Nonetheless, there are few established populations in the state. Though not established, they may be encountered in almost any body of water. Goldfish frequently hybridize with Common Carp through a unique fertilization process; this sometimes forms all-female populations. Brightly colored fish are very susceptible to predation, thus established populations are predominately olive green in color.

Description: olive to silver-white back; cross-hatched sides; large scales with a dark edge and a black spot at base; clear to gray-brown fins; upturned mouth; no barbels near mouth

Similar Species: Bighead Carp (pg. 70), Common Carp (pg. 72), Silver Carp (pg. 78)

Grass Carp	Bighead Carp	Common Carp	Silver Carp
large silver scales with dark margin	small silver scales	large yellow scales with dark margin	small silver scales

Grass Carp	Common Carp
mouth upturned, no barbels	downturned mouth with barbels

GRASS CARP

Ctenopharyngodon idella

Other Names: white amur

Habitat: lakes, ponds and backwaters of large, warm rivers

Range: Asia, introduced in other parts of the world; Missouri—Mississippi, Missouri and Osage Rivers, impoundments and aquaculture ponds

Food: submerged aquatic vegetation, some floating algae

Reproduction: spawns from late spring to early summer, laying over a million eggs in warm, slowly flowing water; eggs remain suspended for several days before hatching

Average Size: 18 to 30 inches; 5 to 30 pounds

Records: State—69 pounds, Crowder State Park, 2002; North American—80 pounds, Lake Wedington, Arkansas, 2004

Notes: Grass Carp were introduced into the US in the 1960s for aquaculture and aquatic vegetation control. By the late `70s, Grass Carp could be found in 40 states. Using Grass Carp for vegetation control is still permitted and popular in many states, including Missouri. Non-breeding triploid fish (fish with three sets of chromosomes instead of the normal two) are frequently used for this purpose. Grass Carp are well established in the Mississippi and Missouri Rivers where they make up a significant portion of the commercial harvest. They are hooked more often than the other Asian carp species, but not consistently enough to be of interest to anglers.

Description: dark-green back; silver sides with a cross-hatched pattern; upturned mouth; eyes far forward and low on head; tiny trout-like scales; no scales on head

Similar Species: Bighead Carp (pg. 70), Common Carp (pg. 72), Grass Carp (pg. 76)

Silver Carp	Bighead Carp	Common Carp	Grass Carp
small silver scales	small silver scales	large yellow scales with dark margin	large silver scales with dark margin

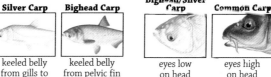

Silver Carp	Bighead Carp	Bighead/Silver Carp	Common Carp
keeled belly from gills to anal fin	keeled belly from pelvic fin to anal fin	eyes low on head	eyes high on head

SILVER CARP

Hypophthalmichthys molitrix

Other Names: shiner carp

Habitat: quiet waters of large, warm rivers and connected lakes and ponds

Range: Asia, introduced in other parts of the world; Missouri—primarily present in the Mississippi and Missouri Rivers

Food: aquatic vegetation, some floating algae

Reproduction: spawns from late spring to early summer in backwaters of large to midsized streams

Average Size: 24 to 36 inches, 5 to 50 pounds

Records: none

Notes: Silver Carp were introduced to Arkansas in the early `70s to control algae in aquaculture ponds and sewage lagoons, then escaped to the Mississippi River. They were first reported in Missouri in 1982. Large breeding populations are well established in the Ohio and Illinois Rivers and their numbers are increasing in the Mississippi and Missouri Rivers. Combined with Bighead Carp, they are the predominant fish in some areas and have a very negative effect on river ecology. The Silver Carp, and to a lesser degree the Bighead Carp, makes high leaps from the water when frightened by boats. As algae feeders, they are targets for bow fishermen, but not anglers. They have limited food value in this country but are an important food source in other parts of the world.

Description: dark-green, blotchy back; sides have two broad lateral bands on a tan background; creamy red between stripes; yellow belly; in breeding males the belly turns bright red; in females, the belly turns yellow-orange but never red; very small scales

Similar Species: Fathead Minnow (pg. 82)

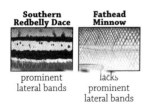

Southern Redbelly Dace	Fathead Minnow
prominent lateral bands	lacks prominent lateral bands

SOUTHERN REDBELLY DACE

Phoxinus erythrogaster

Other Names: redbelly or yellow-belly dace, leatherback

Habitat: small, clear streams with wooded and undercut banks

Range: north-central US with outlying populations in the Ozark Mountain Range; Missouri--the Ozark Region and a few streams along the Mississippi in the northeast

Food: bottom feeders on algae and plant matter

Reproduction: in early summer, a single female is attended by several males and spawns near the bottom in slow-moving pools; eggs hatch in 8 to 10 days without parental care

Average Size: 2 to 3 inches

Records: none

Notes: A small group of minnows are referred to as daces. These small fish are primarily stream dwellers. The brightly colored Southern Redbelly Dace is one of Missouri's most beautiful fish and is well suited as an aquarium fish. If the light is controlled, they will maintain their breeding colors for several months. Dace congregate in tightly packed schools when water levels are low, making them very susceptible to predators and overharvesting for bait.

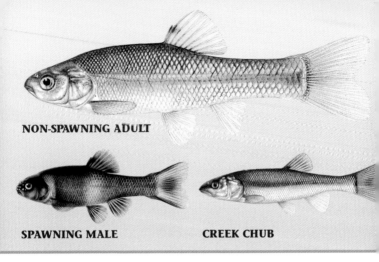

NON-SPAWNING ADULT

SPAWNING MALE

CREEK CHUB

Description: Fathead—olive to slate-gray back; dull yellow sides; dark stripe narrows toward tail then widens to dark spot: Creek Chub—dark-olive back; silver sides with purple sheen; small barbel between upper jaw and snout (very evident with mouth open)

Similar Species: Creek Chub

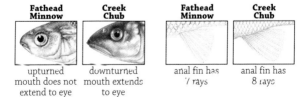

Fathead Minnow	Creek Chub	Fathead Minnow	Creek Chub
upturned mouth does not extend to eye	downturned mouth extends to eye	anal fin has 7 rays	anal fin has 8 rays

FATHEAD MINNOW
Pimephales promelas

CREEK CHUB *Semotilus atromaculatus*

Other Names: Fathead—blackhead, tuffy; Creek Chub— brook or silver chub, horned dace

Habitat: Both—in streams, Fathead—shallow, weedy lakes

Range: US east of Rocky Mountains; Missouri—Creek Chub common throughout; Fathead—common in northern half of state, possible in south of state

Food: Both—small insects and crustaceans, Fathead—more plant matter

Reproduction: Fathead—males build nests beneath rocks and sticks; females lay adhesive eggs on overhang; Creek Chub—males build a teardrop-shaped mound of stones 1 to 2 feet long for a nest then defends it from other males

Average Size: Fathead—3 to 4 inches, Creek Chub— 4 to 10 inches

Records: none

Notes: There are over 1,500 known minnow species in the world, 200 species in the US and about 50 in Missouri. The Fathead and Creek Chub are two of the most widespread minnows native to Missouri. The Fathead is a small minnow that prefers quiet pools and weedy lakes. Creek Chubs are much larger and prefer the moving water of creeks and streams. Both fish are common bait minnows. Fatheads are farmed commercially for bait, but Creek Chubs are caught in the wild and local populations can be easily depleted by overharvesting.

83

Description: back gold to greenish gold; sides golden with silver reflections; belly is yellowish silver; deep slab-sided body; mouth angled up; long triangle-shaped head; lateral line with pronounced downward curve, lowest point above pelvic fins

Similar Species: Creek Chub (pg. 82)

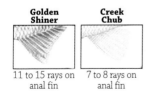

Golden Shiner	Creek Chub
11 to 15 rays on anal fin	7 to 8 rays on anal fin

GOLDEN SHINER
Notemigonus crysoleucas

Cyprinidae

Other Names: bream, American bream, roach, American roach, butterfish, pond shiner

Habitat: clear, weedy ponds and quiet stream waters

Range: native to eastern US south to Florida, introduced in the West; Missouri—common throughout the state

Food: plankton, crustaceans, aquatic insects, mollusks

Reproduction: extended midsummer spawning season; a female attended by one or two males spreads adhesive eggs over submerged vegetation; no parental care

Average Size: 3 to 7 inches

Records: none

Notes: There are almost 20 Missouri minnows called shiners and most are in the genus *Notropis*. Not all shiners are as flashy as the name indicates; some are dull and show almost no bright colors on the sides. The Golden Shiner is a large, showy minnow that congregates in large schools, particularly when young. Sometimes found in open water, but never far from vegetation, Golden Shiners are an important forage species and baitfish. Golden Shiners are native to the rocky streams of Missouri and are now widely propagated and sold for bait. Their range seems to be increasing with introductions from bait pails.

Description: dark-green to dark-blue back and upper sides; bright silver or golden sides; large yellow-tinged eye; large scales; thin body flattened from side to side with a sharp scale ridge (keel) from throat to pelvic fin; forward-facing mouth with small teeth

Similar Species: Mooneye (pg. 88), Herrings/Shads (pp. 56–62)

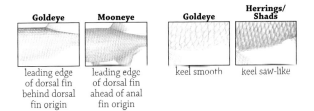

Goldeye	Mooneye	Goldeye	Herrings/Shads
leading edge of dorsal fin behind dorsal fin origin	leading edge of dorsal fin ahead of anal fin origin	keel smooth	keel saw-like

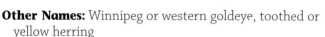

GOLDEYE
Hiodon alosoides

Other Names: Winnipeg or western goldeye, toothed or yellow herring

Habitat: large lakes and quiet backwaters of large, turbid (cloudy) streams and rivers

Range: Hudson Bay drainage south through the Ohio and Mississippi drainages to Tennessee; Missouri—Mississippi, Missouri and Osage Rivers and larger streams in the northeast

Food: insects, small fish, crayfish, snails

Reproduction: spawning takes place in turbid pools and backwaters when water temperatures reach the mid-50s

Average Size: 12 to 18 inches, 1 to 2 pounds

Records: State—1 pounds, 8 ounces, Black River, 2003; North American—3 pounds, 13 ounces, Ohae Tailwater, South Dakota, 1987

Notes: The Goldeye's large yellow eye is an adaptation for low-light conditions and enables it to feed at night and navigate dark, silty waters. They feed near the surface in quiet pools, and are often found with Mooneyes. Harvested commercially from large Canadian lakes for 150 years, they were served on the Canadian Pacific Railway and marketed as Winnipeg Smoked Goldeye. While not often the target of anglers, Goldeyes readily take flies and small lures and are frequently caught while fishing for other species. They are still fairly common in the Mississippi and Missouri Rivers.

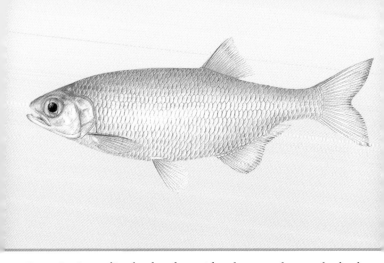

Description: olive back; silver sides; large scales on the body, none on the head; large white eye is over one third the width of the head; thin, flattened body with a sharp, scaleless keel between the pelvic and anal fins; terminal mouth

Similar Species: Herrings/Shads (pp. 56–62), Goldeye (pg. 86)

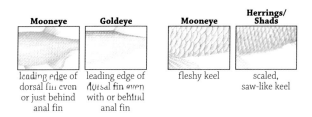

Mooneye	**Goldeye**	**Mooneye**	**Herrings/ Shads**
leading edge of dorsal fin even or just behind anal fin	leading edge of dorsal fin even with or behind anal fin	fleshy keel	scaled, saw-like keel

MOONEYE
Hiodon tergisus

Hiodontidae

Other Names: white shad, slicker, toothed herring, river whitefish

Habitat: clear, quiet waters of large lakes and the backwaters of large streams

Range: Hudson Bay drainage east to the St. Lawrence, through the Mississippi drainage south into Arkansas and Alabama; Missouri—uncommon throughout the state

Food: insects, small fish, crayfish, snails

Reproduction: adults migrate up larger tributaries to spawn in early spring when water temperatures reach the mid-50s; gelatin-coated eggs are released over gravel bars in fast currents

Average Size: 12 inches, 12 ounces to 1 pound

Records: State—13 ounces, Meramec River, 1999; North American—1 pound, 1 ounce, Lake Poygan, Wisconsin, 2000

Notes: Mooneyes are small, flashy fish that commonly feed on insects in the slack waters of large lakes and rivers. They are not as common as Goldeyes in Missouri but are found in the Ozark streams where Goldeyes are absent. Mooneyes are scrappy on light tackle and jump repeatedly when hooked. They are bony with little meat, except along the back and are not good table fare. Though small, they are related to the Arapaima, the world's largest scaled freshwater fish.

89

Description: large, gray body; lacks scales; snout protrudes into a large paddle; shark-like forked tail; gills extend into long, pointed flaps

Similar Species: none

PADDLEFISH
Polyodon spathula

Other Names: spoonbill cat, duckbill

Habitat: deep pools of large rivers and their connecting lakes

Range: large rivers in the Mississippi drainage; Missouri—Mississippi, Missouri and Osage Rivers and impoundments

Food: free-swimming plankton

Reproduction: spawning takes place when water levels are rising in the spring and temperatures reach the low 60s; adults migrate up large tributaries until blocked by dams; breeding schools gather in moving water less than 10 feet deep to release eggs over large gravel bars

Average Size: 2 to 4 feet, 20 to 40 pounds

Records: State—108 pounds, 8 ounces, Lake Jacomo, 1988; North American—144 pounds, Dam #7, Kansas, 2004

Notes: This prehistoric fish is very shark-like in anatomy, with its only close relative found in the Yangtze River of China. Paddlefish have a large mouth but no teeth and feed entirely on plankton. The function of the paddle is not well understood, but it is not used to dig in the mud as once suspected. Scientists believe that sensors in the paddle detect electrical currents created by clouds of plankton. The construction of locks and dams have greatly reduced the Paddlefish population in most of the state. Once an important commercial fish for both meat and caviar, it is now reduced to sport fishing levels that are maintained with some stocking.

Description: tan to olive back and upper sides with dark blotches and speckles; sides tan to golden with X, Y and W patterns; breeding males dark with black bars

Similar Species: Banded Sculpin (pg. 112)

Johnny Darter

scaled body

Banded Sculpin

no scales

JOHNNY DARTER

Etheostoma nigrum

Other Names: black, yellowbelly or weed darter

Habitat: lakes that have some vegetation or algae mats; clear, slow-flowing streams

Range: Rocky Mountains east across Canada and the US through the Great Lakes region; Missouri—common statewide except the southeastern corner and the south-central Ozarks

Food: small aquatic invertebrates

Reproduction: in May and June, males migrate to shorelines to establish breeding areas; females move from territory to territory, spawning with several males; each sequence produces 7 to 10 eggs, which sink and attach to the bottom

Average Size: 2 to 4 inches

Records: none

Notes: There are over thirty darter species found in Missouri. Relatives of the Yellow Perch and Walleye, Darters are primarily stream fish well adapted to living among rocks in fast current. A small swim bladder allows darters to sink rapidly to the bottom after a "dart," thereby avoiding being swept away by the current. Darters are hard to see when they move, but are easy to spot when perched on their pectoral fins. Johnny Darters prefer weedy shorelines in lakes and slow streams, but can be found in a wider range of habitats than most darters.

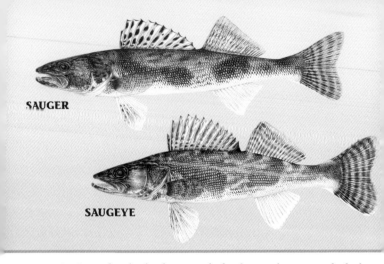

SAUGER

SAUGEYE

Description: slender body; gray, dark silver or brown with dark side blotches; sharp canine teeth; black spots on spiny dorsal; some white on lower tail margin, lacks Walleye's white tail spot

Similar Species: Walleye (pg. 96), Saugeye

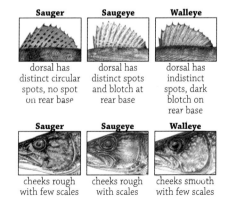

Sauger	Saugeye	Walleye
dorsal has distinct circular spots, no spot on rear base	dorsal has distinct spots and blotch at rear base	dorsal has indistinct spots, dark blotch on rear base

Sauger	Saugeye	Walleye
cheeks rough with few scales	cheeks rough with scales	cheeks smooth with few scales

SAUGER *Sander canadensis*
SAUGEYE *Sander vitreus*

Other Names: sand, spotfin or river pike, jackfish, jack salmon

Habitat: large lakes and rivers

Range: large lakes and rivers in southern Canada, the northern US and the wider reaches of the Mississippi, Missouri, Ohio and Tennessee River drainages; Missouri— Mississippi and Missouri Rivers

Food: small fish, aquatic insects, crayfish

Reproduction: spawns in April and May as the water approaches 50 degrees; adults move into the shallow waters of small tributaries and headwaters to randomly deposit eggs over gravel beds

Average Size: 10 to 12 inches, 8 ounces to 2 pounds

Records: State—5 pounds, 1 ounce; Osage River, 1994; North American—8 pounds, 12 ounces, Lake Sakakawea, North Dakota, 1971

Notes: Though the Sauger is the Walleye's smaller cousin, it is a big-water fish primarily found in large lakes and rivers. It is slow growing and often reaches only two pounds in twenty years in cold water. The Sauger populations in the Mississippi and Missouri Rivers are still strong, but saugers are rare in other Missouri rivers and absent from the large reservoirs. Saugers are aggressive daytime feeders compared to Walleye. Saugeyes are Walleye-Sauger hybrids found both in nature and produced in hatcheries. Both have fine, flavored flesh that is top table fare.

95

Description: long, round body; dark silver or golden- to dark-olive brown in color; spines in both first dorsal and anal fin; sharp canine teeth; dark spot at base of the last three spines of the dorsal fin; white spot on bottom lobe of tail

Similar Species: Sauger (pg. 94), Saugeye (pg. 94)

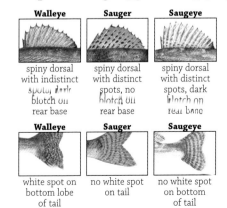

Walleye	Sauger	Saugeye
spiny dorsal with indistinct spots, dark blotch on rear base	spiny dorsal with distinct spots, no blotch on rear base	spiny dorsal with distinct spots, dark blotch on rear base

Walleye	Sauger	Saugeye
white spot on bottom lobe of tail	no white spot on tail	no white spot on bottom of tail

WALLEYE

Sander vitreus

Other Names: marble-eyes, walleyed pike, jack, jackfish, Susquehanna salmon

Habitat: lakes and streams; abundant in some large lakes

Range: native to the northern states and Canada, now widely stocked throughout the US; Missouri—large streams and reservoirs throughout the state

Food: mainly small fish, but also eats insects, crayfish and leeches

Reproduction: spawns in tributary streams or on rocky lake shoals when spring water temperatures reach 45-50 degrees; no parental care

Average Size: 14 to 17 inches, 1 to 3 pounds

Records: State—21 pounds, 1 ounce, Bull Shoals Lake, 1988; North American—21 pounds, 11 ounces, Greer's Ferry Lake, Arkansas, 1982

Notes: Revered by anglers, Walleyes are one of the most popular sport fish in Missouri. They are not strong fighters but fine table fare. A reflective layer of pigment in the eye allows Walleyes to see in low-light conditions. As a result, Walleyes are most active at dusk, dawn and under low-light conditions. Saugeyes are Walleye-Sauger hybrids that occasionally occur naturally and are produced in some hatcheries for stocking. Native to the Mississippi and Missouri Rivers, Walleyes are now stocked in large impoundments throughout the state.

Description: 6 to 9 olive-green vertical bars on a yellow-brown background; two separate dorsal fins—the front fin consists entirely of spines, the back fins consist of soft rays; the lower fins are tinged yellow or orange and brighter in breeding males

Similar Species: Walleye (pg. 96), Yellow Bass (pg. 184)

Yellow Perch	Walleye	Yellow Perch	Yellow Bass
lacks prominent white spot on tail	white spot on bottom of tail	vertical bars on sides of body	horizontal stripes on body

YELLOW PERCH

Perca flavescens

Other Names: ringed, striped or jack perch

Habitat: lakes and streams, prefers clear, open water

Range: widely introduced throughout southern Canada and the northern US, Missouri—rare to uncommon, stocked in a few lakes and reservoirs

Food: minnows, insects, snails, leeches and crayfish

Reproduction: spawns at night in shallow, weedy areas when water temperatures reach 45 degrees; females drape gelatinous ribbons of eggs over submerged vegetation

Average Size: 8 to 11 inches, 6 to 10 ounces

Records: State—1 pounds, 11 ounces, Bull Shoals Lake, 2009; North American—4 pounds, 3 ounces, Bordentown, New Jersey, 1865

Notes: Yellow Perch are northern fish that are rare to uncommon in natural lakes associated with the Mississippi and Missouri Rivers. A few man-made lakes and reservoirs have been stocked with perch and now have self-sustaining populations. Perch are primarily lake fish that congregate in large schools and are a popular panfish in many states. Perch have firm white flesh with a flavor similar to Walleye.

Description: olive-green to yellow-brown back and sides; yellow-green chain-like markings on the sides; distinct dark teardrop below the eye; scales on the entire cheek and gill covers; fins almost clear

Similar Species: Grass Pickerel (pg. 102), Northern Pike (pg. 106)

Chain Pickerel	**Grass Pickerel**	**Northern Pike**
bar under eye vertical	bar under eye angled back	no bar under eye

Chain Pickerel	**Grass Pickerel**
chain-like marks on sides	light and dark vertical marks on sides

CHAIN PICKEREL
Esox niger

Other Names: weed, jack or chain pike, jack pickerel

Habitat: shallow, weedy lakes and sluggish streams

Range: eastern US from the Great Lakes and Maine to Florida and west through the Gulf States to Texas; Missouri—southeast Ozark Region

Food: small fish, aquatic invertebrates

Reproduction: spawning takes place in April and May; adhesive eggs are deposited over shallow submerged vegetation and left to hatch with no parental care; occasionally spawns in fall with a very low survival rate

Average Size: 18 to 24 inches, 1 to 3 pounds

Records: State—5 pounds, 1 ounce, Clearwater Spillway, 1974; North American—9 pounds, 6 ounces; Homerville, Georgia, 1961

Notes: The Chain Pickerel is the largest of the pickerels and a respected game fish. Chain Pickerels frequent the outside edges of weedbeds and bite readily on minnow-imitation lures. When fished on light tackle or a fly rod, they put up a good fight. Chain Pickerels have a tendency to stunt when overpopulated, filling lakes and channels with half-pound "hammer handles." All members of the pike family have intramuscular "Y" bones, an adaptation that enables them to lunge suddenly and capture prey. The Chain Pickerel's flesh is flavorful, but their small "Y" bones make them unpopular as table fare.

Description: olive-green to yellow-brown back and sides; wavy yellowish bars on sides; dark teardrop below eye; fins cream to pale yellow; scales on entire cheek and gill covers

Similar Species: Chain Pickerel (pg. 100) Northern Pike (pg. 106)

Grass Pickerel	**Chain Pickerel**	**Northern Pike**
bar under eye angled back	bar under eye vertical	no bar under eye

Grass Pickerel	**Chain Pickerel**
light and dark vertical marks on sides	chain-like marks on sides

GRASS PICKEREL

Esox americanus vermiculatus

Common Names: mud or little pickerel, grass or mud pike

Habitat: shallow, weedy lakes and sluggish streams

Range: eastern one-third of the United States from the Great Lakes basin to Maine and south to Florida and west through the Gulf states; Missouri—common in southeast Missouri and uncommon in southeastern Ozarks, rare in Mississippi River

Food: small fish, aquatic insects

Reproduction: spawns in early spring; adults enter flooded meadows and shallow bays to lay eggs in less than 2 feet of water; adhesive eggs are deposited over shallow, submerged vegetation; no parental care

Size: 10 to 12 inches, under 1 pound

Records: State—1 pound, 3 ounces (not recorded as a North American record), farm pond, 2005; North American—1 pound, Dewart Lake, Indiana, 1990

Notes: The Grass Pickerel is the smallest member of the pike family and inhabits the dense vegetation in slow-moving streams and smaller lakes. Grass Pickerels readily take small lures and minnows and are often caught by anglers who think they've caught baby pike. They are too small to be of interest to anglers and at times can be a nuisance for panfish anglers. Grass Pickerels are reasonably common in streams and ditches in southeastern Missouri that have good vegetation.

MUSKELLUNGE

TIGER MUSKIE

Description: torpedo-shaped body; dorsal fin near tail; dark gray-green back; silver to silver-green sides; dark vertical bars or blotches on sides (dark markings on light background); tail lobes pointed

Similar Species: Grass Pickerel (pg. 102), Northern Pike (pg. 106)

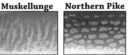

Muskellunge	Northern Pike
dark marks on light background	light marks on dark background

Muskellunge	Northern Pike
6 or more pores on each side under the jaw	5 or fewer pores on each side under the jaw

Muskellunge	Grass Pickerel	Northern Pike	Tiger Muskie
pointed tail	rounded tail	rounded tail	rounded tail

MUSKELLUNGE
Esox masquinongy

Other Names: muskie, Great Lakes or Ohio Muskellunge

Habitat: waters of large, clear, weedy lakes; medium to large rivers with slow currents and deep pools

Range: the Great Lakes basin east to Maine, south through the Ohio River drainage to Tennessee; Missouri—stocked in a few lakes and reservoirs

Food: small fish

Reproduction: spawning takes place in late spring when the water temperature reaches 50 to 60 degrees; eggs are laid in dead vegetation in tributary streams or shallow bays

Average Size: 30 to 42 inches, 10 to 20 pounds

Records: State—41 pounds, 2 ounces, Lake of the Ozarks, 1981; North American—69 pounds, 11 ounces, Chippewa Flowage, Wisconsin, 1949; Missouri Tiger Muskie—22 pounds, Stockton Lake, 1886

Notes: The Muskellunge is the prize of all freshwater game fishing. This large, fast predator prefers large, shallow, clear lakes. They are hard to entice with lures or bait, and muskie fishermen average over 50 hours to catch a legal fish. Muskies are northern fish that are not native to Missouri, but they have been stocked in several large lakes. Muskellunge readily hybridize with Northern Pike (producing Tiger Muskellunge) and pure muskie stock in natural populations is rare. Tiger Muskies are easier to rear than pure muskies and are often preferred for stocking programs.

Description: dark-green back; light-green sides with bean-shaped light spots on a dark background; elongated body with a dorsal fin near the tail; head is long and flattened in front, forming a duck-like snout

Similar Species: Grass Pickerel (pg. 102), Muskellunge (pg. 104), Tiger Muskie (pg. 104)

Northern Pike	Muskellunge	Northern Pike	Muskellunge
rounded tail	pointed tail	5 or fewer pores on under side of jaw	6 or more pores on each side under the jaw

Northern Pike	Grass Pickerel	Muskellunge	Tiger Muskie
light spots on dark background	chain-like marks on sides	dark marks on light background	dark marks on light background

NORTHERN PIKE
Esox lucius

Other Names: great northern pickerel, jack or jackfish, hammerhandle, snot rocket

Habitat: lakes and slow-moving streams, often associated with vegetation

Range: northern Europe, Asia, and North America; Missouri—uncommon to rare in Osage, Mississippi and Missouri Rivers, stocked in a few reservoirs

Food: small fish, occasionally frogs, crayfish

Reproduction: in early spring as water temperatures reach 34 to 40 degrees, eggs are laid among shallow vegetation in tributary streams or lake edges; no parental care

Average Size: 18 to 24 inches, 2 to 5 pounds

Records: State—18 pounds, 9 ounces; Stockton Lake, 1975; North American—46 pounds, 2 ounces, Great Sacandaga Lake, New York, 1940

Notes: This large, fast predator is one of the most wide-spread freshwater fish in the world and a prime sport fish throughout its range. Its long, tube-shaped body and intramuscular bones are adaptations for quick bursts of speed. Pike are sight feeders and hunt by lying in wait and capture their prey with a lightning-fast lunge. Many anglers have lost their catch near the boat when the pike employed this burst of speed to escape. Northern Pike are native to Missouri's large rivers, but were rare originally. With stocking, they are now becoming more widespread. The Tiger Muskellunge is a Northern Pike-Muskellunge hybrid. **107**

Description: golden-brown to dark-olive back and sides; creamy-white to orange belly; spots on sides, dorsal fin and sometimes upper lobe of tail; few red spots with light halos

Similar Species: Rainbow Trout (pg. 110)

Brown Trout	**Rainbow Trout**
orange or reddish spots	reddish-pink longitudinal stripe

Brown Trout	**Rainbow Trout**
squared tail, spots faint or absent	forked tail, prominent dark spots

Brown Trout	**Rainbow Trout**
9 rays on anal fin	10–12 rays on anal fin

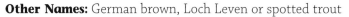

Salmon Family

Salmonidae

BROWN TROUT

Salmo trutta

Other Names: German brown, Loch Leven or spotted trout

Habitat: open ocean near spawning streams and clear, cold, gravel-bottomed streams; shallow portions of the Great Lakes

Range: native to Europe from the Mediterranean to Arctic Norway and Siberia, introduced worldwide; Missouri—stocked in some Ozark streams and reservoirs

Food: insects, crayfish, small fish

Reproduction: spawns October-December in headwater streams, tributaries and stream mouths when migration is blocked; female fans out saucer-shaped nest that male guards until spawning; female covers eggs

Average Size: 11 to 20 inches, 2 to 6 pounds

Records: State—28 pounds, 12 ounces, Lake Taneycomo, 2009; North American—40 pounds, 4 ounces, Little Red River, Arkansas, 1992

Notes: This European trout was brought to North America in the late 1800s; in the east it soon replaced the Brook Trout in many streams. Browns were first stocked in Missouri in the 1920s and 30s. Brown Trout populations are not self-sustaining in Missouri and are maintained through stocking. Brown Trout prefer cold, clear streams but do well in some impoundments. Prized by fly-fishermen the world over, this trout is a secretive, hard-to-catch fish that has a fine, delicate flavor. Brown Trout often aggressively feed on cloudy, rainy days and at night.

109

Description: blue-green to brown head and back; silver lower sides with pink to rose stripes; entire body covered with small black spots; adipose fin

Similar Species: Brown Trout (pg. 108)

reddish-pink longitudinal stripe

orange or reddish spots

forked tail, prominent dark spots

squared tail, spots faint or absent

10–12 rays on anal fin

9 rays on anal fin

RAINBOW TROUT

Oncorhynchus mykiss

Salmonidae

Other Names: steelhead, Pacific, Kamloops or silver trout

Habitat: prefers whitewater in cool streams and coastal regions of large lakes; tolerates smaller cool, clear lakes

Range: Pacific Ocean and coastal streams from Mexico to Alaska and northeastern Russia, introduced world-wide, including in the Great Lakes and in the eastern US; Missouri—introduced in the Ozark Region

Food: insects, small crustaceans, fish

Reproduction: predominantly spring spawners, but some fall spawning varieties exist; female builds nest in well-aerated gravel in both streams and lakes

Average Size: 10 to 15 inches, 1 to 2 pounds

Records: State—18 pounds, 1 ounce, Roaring River, 2004; North American—42 pounds, 2 ounces, Bell Island, Alaska, 1970

Notes: The Rainbow Trout is one of the most widely stocked sport fish around the world. The first attempts to stock this Pacific trout in Missouri were made in the late 1800s and stocking efforts have continued to the present day. There are only a few self-sustaining Rainbow populations in Missouri; virtually all of the trout caught in Missouri are hatchery raised. Rainbow Trout require cold water and are well suited to Ozark streams. Rainbow Trout that migrate from spawning streams into the open ocean or large lakes for part of their life are referred to as Steelheads.

111

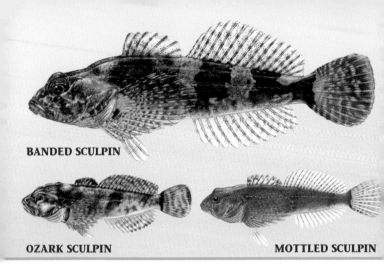

BANDED SCULPIN

OZARK SCULPIN

MOTTLED SCULPIN

Description: rusty brown body with four dark saddles; belly cream colored with dark specks; brown spots on dorsal fin; large, wing-like pectoral fins; white pectoral fins; large mouth; eyes set almost on top of the head; lacks scales

Similar Species: Ozark and Mottled Sculpin

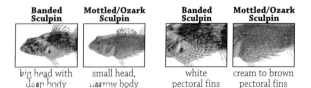

Banded Sculpin	Mottled/Ozark Sculpin	Banded Sculpin	Mottled/Ozark Sculpin
big head with deep body	small head, narrow body	white pectoral fins	cream to brown pectoral fins

SCULPINS
Cottus

Species Names: Banded Sculpin, Mottled Sculpin, Ozark Sculpin

Habitat: cool, swift, hard-bottom streams or rocky or vegetated lakeshore

Range: the Ozark Region through the southern Ohio River drainage, south through the Mobile Bay drainage; Missouri—Ozark Region

Food: aquatic invertebrates, fish eggs, small fish

Reproduction: spawns in late spring when water temperatures reach 63 to 73 degrees; male builds a nest under a ledge, a log or a stream bank then entices the female with elaborate courtship displays; females turn upside down to deposit eggs on "roof" of nest; male tends to nest

Average Size: 2 to 5 inches

Records: none

Notes: Sculpins are fish of cool, fast streams that inhabit the same waters as Rainbow and Brown Trout. The Banded Sculpin can tolerate somewhat warmer water than trout and the other Missouri Sculpins. Frightening-looking fish, the sculpins are perfectly harmless and provide forage for many top predators. In fact, sculpins are a preferred baitfish for large Brown Trout. There are three species of sculpins found in Missouri; the Banded is the most widespread. Though not as common, the Ozark and Mottled Sculpins can be very abundant locally.

113

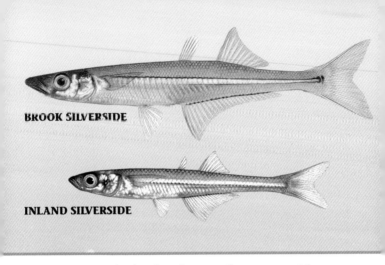

BROOK SILVERSIDE

INLAND SILVERSIDE

Description: sides bright silver to silver-green with conspicuous light stripe; long thin body; upturned mouth; two dorsal fins; tail deeply forked and pointed; the Brook Silverside has 22–25 rays in the anal fin; the Inland only has 15–20

Similar Species: Inland Silverside

Brook Silverside — two dorsal fins, no adipose fin

Inland Silverside — one dorsal fin, adipose fin

BROOK SILVERSIDE

Labidesthes sicculus

Atherinidae

Other Names: northern silverside, skipjack, friar

Habitat: surface areas of clear lakes; slack water of large streams

Range: Great Lake states and the central US south to the Gulf of Mexico; Missouri—common in the Ozark Region through the southeast and the tributaries of the Mississippi River in the northeast

Food: aquatic and flying insects, spiders

Reproduction: spawns in late spring and early summer; eggs are laid in sticky strings that are attached to vegetation

Average Size: 3 to 4 inches

Records: none

Notes: There are two species of Silversides found in Missouri, the Brook and the Inland Silverside. The Brook Silverside is widespread in the Ozark Region, while the Inland Silverside is restricted to the Mississippi River. Both are members of a large family of tropical and subtropical fish, most of which are marine fish. Silversides are flashy fish that are often seen cruising near the lake surface in small schools. Its upturned mouth is an adaptation to surface feeding. It's not uncommon to see Silversides leap from the water, flying-fish style, in pursuit of prey. Silversides have short lifespans, lasting only about 15 months. These sight-feeders seem to become listless and feed less at night and when the water becomes turbid.

115

Description: dark-gray to black back; slate-gray to gray-green sides; bony plates on skin; shark-like tail, with upper lobe longer than lower with no filament; blunt snout with four barbels; spiracles (openings between eye and corner of gill)

Similar Species: Shovelnose Sturgeon (pg. 118), Pallid Sturgeon (pg. 118)

Lake Sturgeon

Pallid/ Shovelnose Sturgeon

spiracle between eye and gill

lacks spiracles

Lake Sturgeon

Pallid/ Shovelnose Sturgeon

no filament on upper lobe of tail

long filament on upper lobe of tail

LAKE STURGEON
Acipenser fulvescens

Other Names: rock, stone, red, black or smoothback sturgeon

Habitat: quiet waters in large rivers and lakes

Range: Hudson Bay, Great Lakes, Mississippi and Missouri drainages southeast to Alabama; Missouri—Mississippi and Missouri Rivers

Food: snails, clams, crayfish, aquatic insects

Reproduction: spawns from April through June in lake shallows and tributary streams; up to 1 million eggs are laid and then fertilized a few at a time

Average Size: 3 to 5 feet, 5 to 40 pounds

Records: State (closed)—53 pounds, Missouri River, 1950; North American—168 pounds, Nattawasaga Lake, Ontario, 1982

Notes: Sturgeons are one of the most primitive fish alive today, with relatives back more than 350 million years. They are bottom-feeders that require clear, clean, deep lakes or river pools. They mature slowly, taking between ten and twenty years before they spawn first. Lake Sturgeon over three hundred pounds and a hundred years old have been reported in southern Canada. Lake Sturgeon were once common in Missouri's large rivers and were commercially fished, but today they are endangered. There have been some attempts in recent years to reestablish the Lake Sturgeon in Missouri.

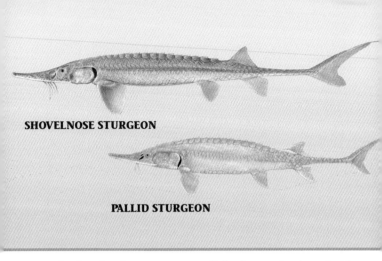

SHOVELNOSE STURGEON

PALLID STURGEON

Description: both copper-tan to light-brown back and sides; long flat snout; bony plates instead of scales; shark-like tail, long upper lobe ending in long filament; Pallid–base of outer barbels behind base of inner barbels; Shovelnose–base of outer barbels even with inner barbels

Similar Species: Lake Sturgeon (pg. 116)

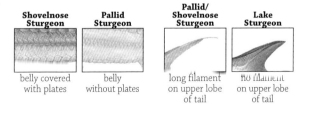

Shovelnose Sturgeon	Pallid Sturgeon	Pallid/ Shovelnose Sturgeon	Lake Sturgeon
belly covered with plates	belly without plates	long filament on upper lobe of tail	no filament on upper lobe of tail

SHOVELNOSE STURGEON

Scaphirhynchus platorynchus

Acipenseridae

PALLID STURGEON *Scaphirhynchus albus*

Other Names: hackleback, sand sturgeon, switchtail

Habitat: open, flowing channels of rivers and large streams with sand or gravel bottoms

Range: Shovelnose—Hudson Bay south through the central US west to New Mexico and east into Kentucky; Pallid—main channels of Missouri and Mississippi Rivers from Montana to Louisiana; Missouri—Missouri and Mississippi Rivers and a few large tributaries

Food: clams, snails, crayfish, insects

Reproduction: spawns in spring when water temperatures reach 65 to 70 degrees; adults migrate upriver to dams or into small tributaries; eggs are deposited in swift current over gravel bars; spawns below dams when necessary

Average Size: 2 feet, 3 pounds

Records: State (Shovelnose)—4 pounds, Des Moines River, 2001; North American—8 pounds, 5 ounces, Rock River, Illinois, 1998

Notes: These small sturgeons are both large-river fish that prefer moving water with a sand or gravel bottom. The Shovelnose Sturgeon is still common enough in the Missouri and Mississippi Rivers to be netted commercially for its meat and eggs, which produce caviar. The Pallid Sturgeon was never as plentiful as the Shovelnose and is now rare and endangered.

Description: olive-brown to bronze back; dull olive-green sides; blunt snout; rounded head; long dorsal fin; large forward-facing mouth with thin lips

Similar Species: Black Buffalo (pg. 122), Smallmouth Buffalo (pg. 124), Common Carp (pg. 72)

Bigmouth Buffalo	**Black Buffalo**	**Smallmouth Buffalo**
upper lip level with lower edge of eye	upper lip well below eye	upper lip well below eye

Bigmouth Buffalo	**Common Carp**
forward-facing mouth, lacks barbels	downturned mouth with barbels

BIGMOUTH BUFFALO
Ictiobus cyprinellus

Other Names: baldpate, blue router, mongrel, prairie or round buffalo, router

Habitat: soft-bottomed shallows of large lakes, sloughs and oxbows; slow-flowing rivers and streams

Range: Saskatchewan to Lake Erie south through the Mississippi River drainage to the Gulf of Mexico; Missouri—common statewide

Food: small mollusks, aquatic insect larvae, zooplankton

Reproduction: spawns in early spring in clear, shallow water in flooded fields and marshes when water temperatures reach the low 60s; young quickly return to main lake or river when water recedes

Average Size: 18 to 20 inches, 10 to 12 pounds

Records: State—56 pounds, Loch-Loma Lake, 1976; North American—73 pounds, 1 ounce; Lake Koshkonong, Wisconsin, 2004

Notes: This large, schooling fish is a filter feeder and commercially harvested with nets in the Mississippi and Missouri Rivers, but it is not often taken on hook and line. Bigmouth Buffalo can tolerate low oxygen levels, high water temperatures and some turbidity, but prefer to forage in clean, clear water. This large, strong fighter is good to eat and would be a world-class sport fish if it would more readily take a hook.

Description: slate-green to dark-gray back; sides have a blue-bronze sheen; deep body with a sloping back that supports a long dorsal fin; upper lip well below eye

Similar Species: Bigmouth Buffalo (pg. 120), Smallmouth Buffalo (pg. 124), Common Carp (pg. 72)

Black Buffalo

upper lip well below eye

Bigmouth Buffalo

upper lip level with lower edge of eye

Smallmouth Buffalo

upper lip well below eye

Buffalo Species

forward-facing mouth, lacks barbels

Common Carp

downturned mouth with barbels

BLACK BUFFALO

Ictiobus niger

Other Names: buoy tender, round, current or deep-water buffalo

Habitat: deep, fast water of large streams, deep sloughs, backwaters and impoundments

Range: lower Great Lakes and southern Mississippi River drainages west to South Dakota, south to New Mexico and Louisiana; Missouri—uncommon but present throughout state

Food: aquatic insects, crustaceans, algae

Reproduction: spawning takes place in April and May when water reaches the low 60s; adults move up tributary streams to lay eggs in flooded sloughs and marshes

Average Size: 15 to 20 inches, 10 to 12 pounds

Records: State—53 pounds, Wappapello Lake, 1989; North American—63 pounds, 6 ounces, Mississippi River, Iowa, 1999

Notes: The Black Buffalo is a southern species that inhabits the deep, strong currents of large rivers. Large numbers sometimes gather near buoys at the edge of channels. They are common in the Missouri and Mississippi Rivers and were once an important part of the commercial harvest there. They are much less common now and seem to be affected by the invasion of Asian carp. The Black Buffalo can be very abundant locally and though they are not often caught by anglers, they will put up a tremendous fight in fast water.

123

Description: slate-green back with bronze sides; large dark eye; deep laterally compressed body; rounded head; blunt snout; small downturned mouth with thick lips

Similar Species: Black Buffalo (pg. 122), Bigmouth Buffalo (pg. 120), Common Carp (pg. 72)

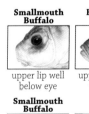

SMALLMOUTH BUFFALO

Ictiobus bubalus

Other Names: razorback, highback or humpback buffalo, thick-lipped buffalo

Habitat: moderate to swift currents in the deep, clean waters of larger streams and some lakes

Range: the Missouri, Mississippi and Ohio River drainages south to the Gulf and west into New Mexico; Missouri—common statewide

Food: small mollusks, aquatic insect larvae and zooplankton

Reproduction: spawns in early spring in clear shallow water of flooded fields and marshes when water temperatures reach the low 60s; young quickly return to main streams when the water recedes

Average Size: 18 to 20 inches, 10 to 12 pounds

Records: State—36 pounds, 12 ounces, Lake of the Ozark, 1986; North American—88 pounds, Lake Wylie, North Carolina, 1993

Notes: The Smallmouth Buffalo is the Bigmouth Buffalo's smaller cousin and is almost as abundant in Missouri, but requires deeper, cleaner water and feeds more heavily on aquatic insect larvae. The Smallmouth Buffalo is commercially harvested and highly respected as table fare. It is often trucked live to markets on the coasts. Few Smallmouth Buffalo are caught by recreational anglers, but they are strong fighters when hooked.

125

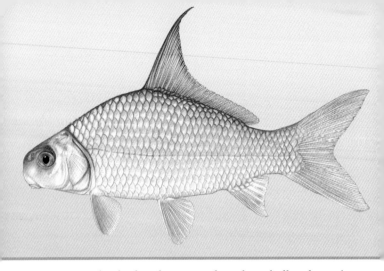

Description: back olive-brown; sides silver; belly white; deep body with hump at dorsal fin; opaque white fins; leading edge of dorsal fin extends into a large, arching "quill"

Similar Species: Common Carp (pg. 72), River Carpsucker (pg. 128), Quillback (pg. 130)

Highfin Carpsucker

no mouth barbels

Common Carp

mouth barbels

Highfin Carpsucker

quill longer than base of dorsal fin

Quillback

quill shorter than base of dorsal fin

River Carpsucker

no quill

HIGHFIN CARPSUCKER

Carpiodes velifer

Other Names: sailfish, skimback, skimfish, humpback or silver carp, spearfish

Habitat: deep water of small to medium clear streams and moderately clear lakes and reservoirs

Range: Ohio and Mississippi River drainage from lower Great Lake States to Gulf; Missouri—rare in central and southern Missouri

Food: aquatic insects, small crustaceans and plant debris

Reproduction: spawns in late spring through mid-summer near tributary stream mouths or dam overflows; adhesive eggs are deposited over gravel in moderate current; eggs are left without parental care

Average Size: 8 to 12 inches, 1 pound

Records: State—open; North American—12 pounds, 10 ounces, Boysen Reservoir, Wyoming, 2005

Notes: Highfin Carpsuckers require cleaner and less turbid water than other carpsuckers and they are becoming rare in Missouri and over most of their range. The largest populations of Highfin Carpsuckers in Missouri occur in the northern Ozarks and the Osage River. Highfins prefer deeper water than Quillbacks and River Carpsuckers but often cruise near the surface with their backs and dorsal fins out of the water. Highfin Carpsuckers are the smallest Missouri carpsucker species and are too rare to be of much interest to Missouri anglers.

Description: olive-brown back; silver sides; fins clear; deep body with round blunt head; high concave dorsal fin; leading edge higher than base of dorsal but not forming single "quill"

Similar Species: Common Carp (pg. 72), Quillback (pg. 130), Highfin Carpsucker (pg. 126)

no mouth barbels

mouth barbels

no quill

quill longer than base of dorsal fin

quill shorter than base of dorsal fin

RIVER CARPSUCKER

Carpiodes carpio

Other Names: white or silver carp, northern carpsucker

Habitat: medium to large rivers with slow current, moderately clear lakes

Range: the Mississippi River drainage from the lower Great Lake States to the Gulf, west to Wyoming and east to Pennsylvania; the Gulf States to Rio Grande Valley; Missouri—common in northern half of the state; occasionally found in southern Missouri

Food: aquatic insects, small crustaceans and plant debris

Reproduction: spawns in late spring to early summer over an extended period; adhesive eggs are spread over moderate vegetation or debris; eggs are left without parental care

Average Size: 11 to 15 inches, 1 to 2 pounds

Records: State—2 pounds, 3 ounces, South Grand River, 2008; North American—7 pounds, 15 ounces, Lake Sharpe, South Dakota, 1999

Notes: The most common carpsucker species, the River Carpsucker frequents medium to large rivers, and is very abundant in some impoundments. They are inactive fish that prefer moderate cover away from the current or nearby shorelines. They feed on the bottom during the day and can be caught by fishing on the bottom using small hooks baited with worms. The can also be caught with wet flies fished slowly on the bottom near cover. Carpsuckers have a good flavor when taken from relatively clean water.

Description: bright silver back and sides, often with yellow tinge; fins clear; deep body with round blunt head; leading edge of dorsal fin extends into a large, arching "quill"

Similar Species: Common Carp (pg. 72), River Carpsucker (pg. 128), Highfin Carpsucker (pg. 126)

no mouth barbels

mouth barbels

Quillback

quill shorter than base of dorsal fin

Highfin Carpsucker

quill longer than base of dorsal fin

River Carpsucker

no quill

QUILLBACK

Carpiodes cyprinus

Other Names: silver carp, carpsucker, lake quillback

Habitat: slow-flowing streams and rivers; backwaters and lakes, particularly areas with soft bottoms

Range: south-central Canada through the Great Lakes to the eastern US, south through the Mississippi drainage to the Gulf; Missouri—common throughout the state

Food: insects, plant matter, decaying material on bottom

Reproduction: spawns in late spring through early summer in tributary streams or lake shallows; eggs are deposited in open areas over sand or mud

Average Size: 12 to 14 inches, 1 to 2 pounds

Records: State—2 pounds, 12 ounces, North Fabius River, 2003; North American—8 pounds, 13 ounces, Lake Winnebago, 2003

Notes: In North America, there are four fish known as carpsuckers. The Quillback is one of three carpsucker species found in Missouri. The other two are the Highfin and River Carpsuckers. All look much alike but are not difficult to tell apart. While Quillbacks and River Carpsuckers are common in Missouri, the Highfin is rare. Carpsuckers prefer medium to large rivers and lakes where they gather in schools to filter-feed along the bottom. Though they are not often sought by anglers, they readily take wet flies and small baited hooks. Quillbacks are good fighters and the flesh is white and very flavorful.

Description: dark, olive back; brassy-gold sides are slightly iridescent green; lower fin is reddish-orange, dark spot at base of scales

Similar Species: Golden Redhorse (pg. 134), River Redhorse (pg. 136), Shorthead Redhorse (pg. 138), Silver Redhorse (pg. 140), White Sucker (pg. 148)

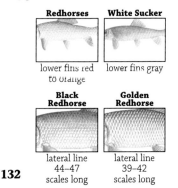

Redhorses
lower fins red to orange

White Sucker
lower fins gray

Black Redhorse
lateral line 44–47 scales long

Golden Redhorse
lateral line 39–42 scales long

BLACK REDHORSE
Moxostoma duquesnei

Other Names: black or finescale mullet, finescale redhorse, blackhorse, black sucker

Habitat: deep pools and runs of small to medium-sized streams; impoundments with good tributary streams

Range: the Great Lakes Region through the Mississippi River Basin to Arkansas; the upper Mobile Bay drainage; Missouri—confined to the Ozark Region

Food: aquatic insects, small crustaceans

Reproduction: spawns in early spring over gravel riffles just below deep pools; males set up territories and make courtship displays with short runs and splashing; females deposit eggs over gravel attended by one or two males

Average Size: 8 to 16 inches, 1 to 2 pounds

Records: State—1 pound, 8 ounces, Meramec River, 1995; North American—1 pound, 14 ounces, French Creek, Pennsylvania, 1997

Notes: The Black Redhorse is a small redhorse species very similar to the Golden Redhorse in appearance and habit. The Black Redhorse prefers deeper pools and runs than the Golden Redhorse. The Black Redhorse is one of the most common fish in small to medium-sized Ozark streams, but in Missouri it is restricted to that region. They are often seen feeding in loose schools in shallow riffles just above deeper pools. Black Redhorses are small and bony but the flesh is firm, white and flavorful.

133

Description: brassy-green to gold back; bronze to golden-green sides; lower fin yellowish-red to dull red; sucker mouth; scale on back and sides with dark spot at base

Similar Species: Black Redhorse (pg. 132), River Redhorse (pg. 136), Shorthead Redhorse (pg. 138), Silver Redhorse (pg. 140), White Sucker (pg. 148)

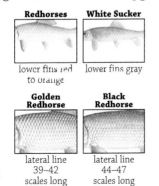

Redhorses
lower fins red to orange

White Sucker
lower fins gray

Golden Redhorse
lateral line 39–42 scales long

Black Redhorse
lateral line 44–47 scales long

GOLDEN REDHORSE

Moxostoma erythrurum

Other Names: golden or smallheaded mullet, golden sucker

Habitat: clean streams and rivers with hard bottoms; rarely, clear lakes with strong tributary streams

Range: Great Lake states to New England south to the Gulf; Missouri—Ozark Region and northeast Missouri

Food: aquatic insects, small crustaceans and plant debris

Reproduction: spawns in tributary streams in early spring when water temperature reaches the low 60s, males build nest and court with much flourish

Average Size: 12 to 20 inches, 2 to 5 pounds

Records: State—5 pounds, 1 ounce, Niangua River, 2004 (not recorded as North American record); North American— 3 pounds, 15 ounces, Root River, Minnesota, 2007

Notes: Golden Redhorses prefer small, clean streams with deep pools separated by riffles. They tolerate warmer water and more turbidity than some of the other small redhorse species, but like other redhorses, they do not withstand pollution well. The Golden Redhorse is one of the most common redhorse species in the Ozark streams, and along with the Shorthead, it is the only redhorse species common in the Mississippi tributary streams in northeast Missouri. Golden Redhorses can be caught with bait and wet flies.

Description: olive-brown to brown back; sides dull silver to bronze; bright red tail; reddish lower fins; blunt nose; 12–13 rays in dorsal fin

Similar Species: Black Redhorse (pg. 132), Golden Redhorse (pg. 134), Shorthead Redhorse (pg. 138), Silver Redhorse (pg. 140), White Sucker (pg. 148)

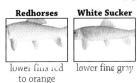

Redhorses
lower fins red to orange

White Sucker
lower fins gray

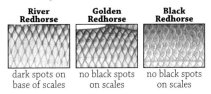

River Redhorse
dark spots on base of scales

Golden Redhorse
no black spots on scales

Black Redhorse
no black spots on scales

136

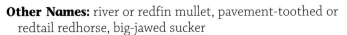

RIVER REDHORSE
Moxostoma carinatum

Other Names: river or redfin mullet, pavement-toothed or redtail redhorse, big-jawed sucker

Habitat: clean streams and rivers with hard bottoms and deep pools; a few clear lakes

Range: Great Lake states to New England south to the Gulf; Missouri—Ozark Region

Food: clams, muscles and other small crustaceans, aquatic insects

Reproduction: spawns in small tributary streams in early spring; males build a nest 4 to 8 feet in diameter over shallow gravel, then court females by darting across nest; second male may join in the display and spawning

Average Size: 12 to 24 inches, 2 to 7 pounds

Records: State—9 pounds, 10 ounces, Osage River, 2006 (not recorded as a North American record); North American—8 pounds, 11 ounces, Trent River, Ontario, 1997

Notes: The River Redhorse inhabits large to medium streams throughout the Ozarks and is the largest Missouri Redhorse species. They have strong pharyngeal teeth (teeth in the throat), which are an adaptation for crushing snails and clams. Like the other redhorse species, they require clean water with a hard substrate and decline in numbers with increased siltation. Due to their large size, River Redhorses are more frequently sought by anglers than other redhorse species.

137

Description: back brassy, green or gold; bronze, gold or green sides; lower fins are yellow-orange to red; blunt nose with a sucker mouth; sickle-shaped dorsal fin

Similar Species: Black Redhorse (pg. 132), Golden Redhorse (pg. 134), River Redhorse (pg. 136)

Shorthead Redhorse

head small and slightly pointed

River Redhorse

large head with a blunt snout

Shorthead Redhorse

dark spots on base of scales

Golden Redhorse

no black spots on scales

Black Redhorse

no black spots on scales

138

SHORTHEAD REDHORSE

Moxostoma macrolepidotum

Other Names: northern, golden, silver, greater, black or river redhorse

Habitat: clean streams and rivers with hard bottoms, and clear lakes with strong-flowing tributary streams

Range: Central Canada and the US through Atlantic States; Missouri—common statewide

Food: aquatic insects, small crustaceans and plant debris

Reproduction: spawns when the water reaches low 60s; adults migrate into small tributary streams to lay eggs on shallow gravel bars in swift currents near deep-water pools

Average Size: 18 to 24 inches, 2 to 5 pounds

Records: State—2 pounds, 14 ounces, Truman Lake, 2009; North American—11 pounds, 5 ounces, Brunet River, Wisconsin, 1983

Notes: The Shorthead Redhorse is the most common and widespread Redhorse species in Missouri. It prefers fast water with a hard bottom in large to medium streams but it is present in a few lakes. The Shorthead Redhorse is common in the Mississippi River and present but less common in the Missouri River. Shortheads look like all the other redhorses but each is a separate species and occupies its own ecological niche. They are not an important sport fish, but they are caught fairly often by river anglers.

Description: dark-gray back, silver sides; lower fins reddish brown (red in breeding season); sucker mouth; no dark spot on back and side scales

Similar Species: Black Redhorse (pg. 132), Golden Redhorse (pg. 134), River Redhorse (pg. 136), Shorthead Redhorse (pg. 138), White Sucker (pg. 148)

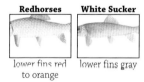

Redhorses	White Sucker
lower fins red to orange	lower fins gray

Silver Redhorse	Other Redhorses
dorsal fin curved, 14–15 rays	dorsal fin slightly concave, 12–13 rays

SILVER REDHORSE

Moxostoma anisurum

Other Names: silver, bay, or redfin mullet, whitenose red-horse, longtail sucker

Habitat: clean streams and rivers with hard bottoms and deep pools; a few clear lakes; shoals of Lake Michigan

Range: Manitoba to the St. Lawrence drainage south to northern Alabama and Missouri; Missouri—the northern and eastern portions of the Ozark Region

Food: aquatic insects, small crustaceans and plant debris

Reproduction: spawns in early spring when the water temperature reaches the high 50s; adults migrate into small tributary streams to lay eggs on shallow gravel bars in the swift current near deep-water pools

Average Size: 11 to 22 inches, 2 to 5 pounds

Records: State—5 pounds, 10 ounces, Sac River, 2000; North American—11 pounds, 5 ounces, Brunet River, Wisconsin, 1983

Notes: Silver Redhorses inhabit the large to medium streams in the eastern and southern Ozarks. They can be very abundant locally but are not normally common. They prefer deep pools and are readily caught when fished with worms on the bottom. The other redhorses are similar in appearance, but each is a separate species and occupies its own niche. Each redhorse has a distinctive lip shape and can be easily told apart. All redhorses require clean water with a hard substrate, and they are declining in numbers with increased siltation. Redhorses are bony but have firm, flavorful flesh. **141**

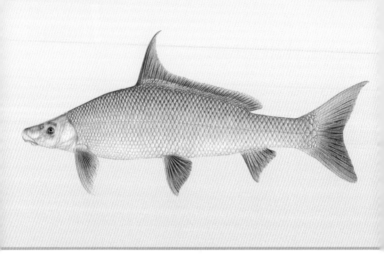

Description: back and sides are blue to blue-gray and blue-white below; small, pointed head with a bulbous snout that overhangs its small mouth; sickle-shaped dorsal fin; deeply forked tail

Similar Species: White Sucker (pg. 148), Spotted Sucker (pg. 146)

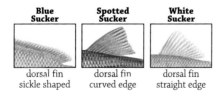

Blue Sucker	Spotted Sucker	White Sucker
dorsal fin sickle shaped	dorsal fin curved edge	dorsal fin straight edge

BLUE SUCKER
Cycleptus elongatus

Other Names: Missouri, slenderheaded, gourdseed, razorback, or sweet sucker

Habitat: deep chutes with strong currents and gravel bottoms in large rivers, deep river impoundments

Range: Mississippi River basin, Gulf states from Louisiana to Rio Grande; Missouri—Mississippi and Missouri Rivers and lower reaches of large tributaries

Food: crustaceans, aquatic insects, some plant material

Reproduction: little is known; spring spawning runs over gravel bars in tributary streams have been noted

Average Size: 12 to 18 inches, 1 to 3 pounds

Records: State—9 pounds, 14 ounces, Missouri River, 1997; North American—14 pounds, 3 ounces, Mississippi River, Minnesota, 1987

Notes: The Blue Sucker is a big-water fish that prefers deep, fast water over a clean gravel bottom. Due to the construction of dams and increasing silt from agricultural fields, there has been less suitable habitat for Blue Suckers, and their numbers have been declining for years. There is some indication the population is rebounding thanks to improving conditions in the Mississippi River. It is reported the Blue Sucker is a fine food fish and the best tasting of all the sucker species. A limited number of Blue Suckers are commercially harvested and sold along the Mississippi River.

Description: back dark olive-brown fading to yellow-brown blotches on sides; 4 to 5 irregular dark saddles; elongated body almost round in cross-section; large head that is concave between the eyes; lower fins are light brown

Similar Species: Redhorses (pg. 132–140), White Sucker (pg. 148), Spotted Sucker (pg. 146)

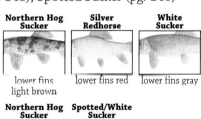

Northern Hog Sucker	Silver Redhorse	White Sucker
lower fins light brown	lower fins red	lower fins gray

Northern Hog Sucker

head concave between eyes

Spotted/White Sucker

head not concave between eyes

NORTHERN HOG SUCKER

Hypentelium nigricans

Other Names: hog molly, hammerhead, riffle or bigheaded sucker, crawl-a-bottom

Habitat: riffles and tailwaters of clear streams with hard bottoms; found in a few lakes near the mouths of tributary streams

Range: central and eastern Canada and the US south to Alabama and west to Oklahoma; Missouri—common in the Ozark Region

Food: small crustaceans, aquatic insects

Reproduction: spawns when water temperature reaches the low 60s; males gather in riffles or pools; females shed eggs that are fertilized by several males; no parental care

Average Size: 8 to 14 inches, 1 to 2 pounds

Records: State—3 pounds, 5 ounces, Current River, 1988 (not recorded as North American record); North American—1 pound, 12 ounces, Fox River, Wisconsin, 2004

Notes: Northern Hog Suckers are clean-water fish that are well adapted to feed in moving water. They use their elongated body structure and concave head to hold their place in riffles while turning over stones to release food. It is common for other fish to follow Hog Suckers, feeding on what is stirred up. Northern Hog Suckers are one of the most common and widespread fish in Ozark streams, but they are declining over much of their range. Hog Suckers are of not much interest to anglers but are sometimes caught by fishermen working the edges of fast water.

Description: dark-green to olive-brown back; sides coppery-green with 8 to 12 rows of dark spots, no lateral line, creamy white lower fins with a dark margin on the dorsal fin and the tip of lower lobe of the tail fin

Similar Species: Northern Hog Sucker (pg. 144), White Sucker (pg. 148)

Spotted Sucker	White Sucker		Spotted Sucker	White Sucker
black on dorsal and tail fin	no black on dorsal and tail fin		no lateral line, rows of spots	lateral line, no spots

Spotted/White Sucker	Northern Hog Sucker
head not concave between eyes	head concave between eyes

SPOTTED SUCKER

Minytrema melanops

Catostomidae

Other Names: spotted redhorse, corncob, striped, speckled and winter sucker

Habitat: long, deep pools of small to medium-sized streams with low gradient and good vegetation, large rivers and impoundments

Range: the lower Great Lakes and the Mississippi River Basin; the Atlantic and Gulf Slope states to the Colorado River Basin; Missouri—common in southeast lowlands, scattered in the Ozarks

Food: insects, crustaceans

Reproduction: spawns in early spring; males defend territories in riffles with much jumping and splashing; female heads upstream with a male on each side as they release eggs and milt over gravel

Average Size: 8 to 14 inches, $\frac{1}{2}$ to $1\frac{1}{2}$ pound

Records: State (snagging, line open)—2 pounds, 1 ounce, Wappapello Lake, 1992; North American—1 pound, 6 ounces, Catfish Creek, Texas, 2002

Notes: The Spotted Sucker is found throughout the Missouri lowlands and occasionally in Ozark streams, but not in the Mississippi River. Farther north in Iowa and Wisconsin, it is common in the big rivers and some floodplain lakes and impoundments. Spotted Suckers prefer slow streams with a soft bottom covered in plant debris. In the clearer Ozark streams it inhabits the backwaters and overflow ponds. Spotted suckers are very tasty when smoked. **147**

Description: back olive to brown; sides gray to silver; belly off-white; slate dorsal and tail fin; lower fins are tinged orange; snout barely extends beyond upper lip; breeding males develop black or purple stripe

Similar Species: Spotted Sucker (pg. 146), Northern Hog Sucker (pg. 144)

White Sucker
no black on dorsal and tail fin

Spotted Sucker
black on dorsal and tail fin

White Sucker
lateral line, no spots

Spotted Sucker
no lateral line, rows of spots

White/Spotted Sucker
head not concave

Northern Hog Sucker
head concave

Catostomidae

WHITE SUCKER
Catostomus commersonii

Other Names: common, coarse-scaled or eastern sucker, bay fish, black mullet

Habitat: clear to slightly turbid (cloudy) streams; rivers and lakes

Range: Canada throughout the east-central US and south from New Mexico to South Carolina; Missouri—statewide except the southeast corner

Food: insects, crustaceans, plant material

Reproduction: spawns in early spring when water reaches the high 50s to low 60s; adults spawn in tributary riffles over gravel or coarse sand; in lakes, eggs are deposited over shallow gravel or rocks along waveswept shorelines

Average Size: 12 to 18 inches, 1 to 3 pounds

Records: State—4 pounds, 8 ounces, Lake Taneycomo, 1990; North American—7 pounds, 4 ounces, Big Round Lake, Wisconsin, 1978

Notes: The White Sucker is found widely throughout Missouri except in the southeast, but in many areas it is not very common. Where it is common, it is highly productive, and provides a large source of forage for game fish. White suckers can thrive in most Missouri streams, even those in the agricultural areas that are heavily silted. There is a large population of White Suckers in Lake Taneycomo. White Suckers have firm, good-tasting flesh that is prized by some when smoked.

149

Description: dark-green back; greenish sides often with a dark lateral band; large forward-facing mouth; lower jaw extends to the rear margin of the eye

Similar Species: Smallmouth Bass (pg. 152), Spotted Bass (pg. 154)

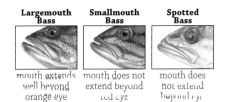

Largemouth Bass	Smallmouth Bass	Spotted Bass
mouth extends well beyond orange eye	mouth does not extend beyond red eye	mouth does not extend beyond eye

LARGEMOUTH BASS

Centrarchidae

Micropterus salmoides

Other Names: black, bayou, green or slough bass, green trout

Habitat: shallow, fertile, weedy lakes and river backwaters; weedy bays of large lakes

Range: southern Canada through the United States into Mexico, extensively introduced throughout the world; Missouri—common statewide

Food: small fish, frogs, crayfish, insects

Reproduction: spawning takes place from April through June when water temperatures reach 60 degrees; male builds a nest in a weedbed less than 6 feet deep; male fans and guards the nest until the "brood swarm" disperses

Average Size: 12 to 20 inches, 1 to 5 pounds

Records: State—13 pounds, 14 ounces, Bull Shoals Lake, 1961; North American—22 pounds, 4 ounces, Montgomery Lake, Georgia, 1932

Notes: The Largemouth Bass is the most sought-after game fish in North America. This denizen of the weeds is a voracious carnivore, eating anything that is alive and will fit into its mouth. Largemouths are native to most of Missouri and have been introduced to any waters that would sustain them. Largemouth Bass often run one to two pounds, with six and seven pounders not uncommon in Missouri. They are quite tasty when small and taken from clean water, but tend to be slightly mud-flavored when taken from silty water.

151

Description: back and sides mottled dark green to bronze or pale gold, often with dark vertical bands; white belly; stout body; large, forward-facing mouth; red eyes

Similar Species: Largemouth Bass (pg. 150), Spotted Bass (pg. 154)

Smallmouth Bass

Largemouth Bass

mouth does not extend beyond red eye

mouth extends well beyond orange eye

Smallmouth Bass

Spotted Bass

vertical bars on sides

lateral stripe on sides

SMALLMOUTH BASS

Micropterus dolomieu

Other Names: bronzeback, redeye bass, redeye, white or mountain trout

Habitat: clear, swift-flowing streams and rivers; clear lakes with gravel or rocky shorelines

Range: introduced throughout North America, Europe and Asia; Missouri—common in the Ozark Region and tributary streams of upper Mississippi River

Food: insects, small fish, crayfish

Reproduction: male builds a nest in 3 to 10 feet of water on open gravel beds when water temperatures reach the mid-to-high 60s; nest is often near a log or boulder; the male aggressively guards the nest and young until fry disperse

Average Size: 12 to 20 inches, 1 to 4 pounds

Records: State—7 pounds, 2 ounces, Stockton Lake, 1994; North American—11 pounds, 15 ounces, Dale Hollow Lake, Tennessee, 1955

Notes: The Smallmouth Bass is a world-class game fish noted for its strong fighting ability and spectacular leaps. Native to the state, it is the primary stream bass in the Ozark Region. There are also good populations in impoundments such as Stockton and Table Rock. The Smallmouth Bass prefers deeper, more open water than its larger cousin, the Largemouth Bass. In streams, it is often found in deep pools at the current's edge. The flesh is firm, succulent, and regarded by many anglers as second only to trout.

153

Description: dark-green back fading to lighter-green sides; diamond-shaped blotches form a dark stripe on the side; dark spots above the stripe; light spots on base of each scale below stripe; dark lines extend from reddish eye

Similar Species: Largemouth Bass (pg. 150), Smallmouth Bass (pg. 152)

Spotted Bass

mouth does not extend beyond eye

Largemouth Bass

mouth extends beyond orange eye

Spotted Bass

spotting below lateral line

Smallmouth Bass

vertical bars on sides

SPOTTED BASS

Micropterus punctulatus

Other Names: Kentucky, speckled or yellow bass, spot

Habitat: deeper silted pools in sluggish, medium-to-large streams; large lakes and reservoirs

Range: the Ohio and Mississippi drainage in the southern US from Florida to Texas; Missouri—the southeastern Missouri lowlands and the western Ozark Region

Food: small fish, crayfish

Reproduction: male builds a nest in open gravel beds three to four feet deep from April through June when water temperatures reach mid-to-high 60s; male aggressively guards the nest and young

Average Size: 8 to 18 inches, 8 ounces to 2 pounds

Records: State—7 pounds, 8 ounces, Table Rock Reservoir, 1966; North American—10 pounds, 4 ounces, Pine Flat Lake, California, 2001

Notes: This bass is primarily a stream fish but has done well in some impoundments. In terms of habits, Spotted Bass fall between Largemouth and Smallmouth Bass. Whereas Smallmouths seek stream riffles and Largemouths prefer the edges of weedbeds, Spotted Bass prefer slow, deep pools. In reservoirs, they seek deeper water than Smallmouth Bass. Spotted Bass are smaller fish than Largemouths but are frequently larger than average Missouri Smallmouth Bass. Spotted Bass frequently hybridize with Smallmouth and in some areas the hybrid is the predominant bass.

Description: black to olive back; silver sides with dark-green to black blotches; its back is more arched and the depression above the eye is more pronounced than in the White Crappie

Similar Species: White Crappie (pg. 158)

Black Crappie	**White Crappie**	**Black Crappie**	**White Crappie**
usually 7 to 8 spines in dorsal fin	usually 5 to 6 spines in dorsal fin	dorsal fin length equal to the distance from the dorsal to the eye	dorsal fin shorter than the distance from the eye to the dorsal

BLACK CRAPPIE

Pomoxis nigromaculatus

Other Names: speck, speckled perch, papermouth

Habitat: quiet, clear water of streams and midsized lakes; often associated with vegetation but may roam deep, open basins and flats, particularly during winter

Range: southern Manitoba through the Atlantic and southeastern states, introduced but not common in the West; Missouri—widespread throughout state

Food: small fish, aquatic insects, zooplankton

Reproduction: spawns in shallow weedbeds from May to June when water temperatures reach the high 50s; male builds circular nest in fine gravel or sand, then guards eggs and young until fry begin feeding

Average Size: 7 to 12 inches, 5 ounces to 1 pound

Records: State—5 pounds, private pond, 2006; North American—6 pounds; Westwego Canal, Louisiana, 1969

Notes: Crappies are the most popular Missouri panfish in all seasons, as they feed actively in both winter and summer. They are sought for their sweet-tasting white fillets, but not for their fighting ability. Black Crappies nest in colonies and often gather in large feeding schools. Widespread in Missouri, Black Crappies are found throughout the state but are not as abundant as White Crappies. Black Crappies require clearer water and more vegetation than White Crappies. Both crappie species are meaty and considered excellent table fare.

157

Description: greenish back; silvery-green to white sides with 7 to 9 dark vertical bars; the only sunfish with six spines in both the dorsal and anal fin

Similar Species: Black Crappie (pg. 156)

White Crappie	Black Crappie	White Crappie	Black Crappie
usually 5 to 6 spines in dorsal fin	usually 7 to 8 spines in dorsal fin	dorsal fin shorter than the distance from the eye to the dorsal	dorsal fin length equal to the distance from the dorsal to the eye

WHITE CRAPPIE

Pomoxis annularis

Other Names: silver, pale or ringed crappie, papermouth

Habitat: slightly silty streams and midsize to large lakes; prefers less vegetation than the Black Crappie

Range: North Dakota south and east to the Gulf and Atlantic states except peninsular Florida; Missouri—statewide

Food: aquatic insects, small fish, plankton

Reproduction: spawns on firm sand or gravel when the water temperature approaches 60 degrees; male builds a shallow, round nest, and guards eggs and young after spawning

Average Size: 8 to 10 inches, 5 ounces to 1 pound

Records: State—4 pounds, 9 ounces, private pond, 2000; North American—5 pounds, 3 ounces, Enid Dam, Mississippi, 1957

Notes: The southern cousin of the Black Crappie, the White Crappie is native to Missouri and common throughout the state. They prefer deeper, less vegetated water than Black Crappies and can thrive with higher turbidity. White Crappies school less than Black Crappies, but where they occur together, they can be found in mixed schools during the winter. Both actively feed during the winter and at night. Crappies are one of the most popular panfish in Missouri and are highly prized for their fine flavor.

Description: body color variable, from dark olive to green on the back, silver-gray, copper, orange, purple or brown on sides; 5 to 9 dark vertical bars on sides that fade with age; yellow belly; copper breast; dark gill spot extends to gill margin; dark spot on rear margin of dorsal fin

Similar Species: Green Sunfish (pg. 166), Redear Sunfish (pg. 172), Longear Sunfish (pg. 168)

Bluegill

small mouth

Green Sunfish

large mouth

Bluegill

dark gill spot

Longear Sunfish

long dark gill flap

Redear Sunfish

red/orange margin on gill

BLUEGILL
Lepomis macrochirus

Other Names: bream, sun perch, blue sunfish, copperbelly, strawberry bass

Habitat: medium to large streams and most lakes with weedy bays or shorelines

Range: southern Canada through the southern states into Mexico; Missouri—abundant throughout state

Food: aquatic insects, snails, small fish

Reproduction: spawns from late May to early August when water temperatures reach the high 60s to low 80s; male builds a nest in shallow, sparse vegetation in a colony of up to 50 other nests; male guards nest and fry

Average Size: 6 to 9 inches, 5 to 12 ounces

Records: State—3 pounds, private pond, 1963; North American—4 pounds, 12 ounces, Ketona Lake, Alabama, 1950

Notes: Bluegills are native to Missouri but historically were not widespread. With extensive introductions they have become common throughout the state. They are one of the most popular panfish in Missouri and in the US. Bluegills prefer impoundments but can be found in most streams that provide protection from the current, and are common in the backwaters of large rivers. Bluegills prefer deep weedbeds at the edge of open water. They have small mouths and feed mostly on insects and small fish frequently on the surface. Many lakes have large populations of hybrid sunfish, which are crosses between Bluegills and Green Sunfish.

161

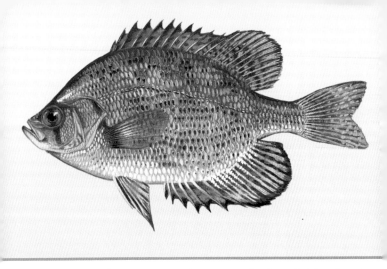

Description: olive-green to silver-green back and sides; longitudinal stripes of brown spots on sides; dark wedge-shaped bar under eye; latterly compressed body; anal and dorsal fin nearly equal length; dark spot on dorsal fin of young fish; small mouth

Similar Species: Crappies (pgs. 156–158), Redspotted Sunfish (pg. 174)

Flier	Crappies
small mouth, dark bar under eye	large mouth, no dark bar under eye

Flier	Redspotted Sunfish
anal and dorsal fin same size	anal fin smaller than dorsal fin

FLIER

Centrarchus macropterus

Other Names: spotfin, silver, round or swamp sunfish

Habitat: quiet, weedy, waters with a soft bottom in lakes, creeks, and coastal swamps

Range: coastal states from Virginia to eastern Texas; the Mississippi Valley through the Ohio Valley to Southern Illinois and Indiana; Missouri—southeast corner

Food: small crustaceans, aquatic insects, zooplankton, small fish

Reproduction: nests in late spring or early summer in dense vegetation; nests are solitary or in small groups, males guard nest and young

Average Size: 4 to 6 inches, four ounces

Records: State—10 ounces, farm pond, 1991; North American—1 pound, 2 ounces, Pope's Pond, Georgia, 1995

Notes: Fliers are small sunfish found only in the southeast lowlands of Missouri. Fliers can withstand low oxygen levels and more acidity than most other sunfish and are very common in still, swampy water. Rarely larger than 6 inches long, Fliers are too small to be an important panfish, but they readily bite and can be proficient bait robbers. When large enough to eat, Fliers have flaky, white flesh and a fine flavor. Fliers are predators of mosquito larvae, and small ones should be carefully returned to the water to help with mosquito control.

163

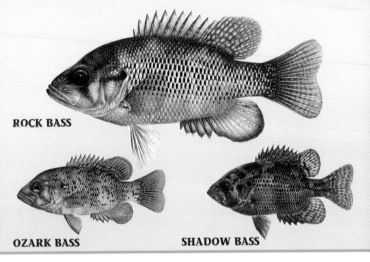

ROCK BASS

OZARK BASS

SHADOW BASS

Description: All—brown to olive-green back and sides with overall bronze appearance; red eye; thicker, heavier body than other sunfish; large mouth; Rock Bass—sides with parallel lines of dark spots; Shadow Bass—sides with broad vertical, dark blotches; Ozark Bass—sides with scattered dark spots

Similar Species: Ozark Bass, Shadow Bass

Rock Bass	Ozark Bass	Shadow Bass
parallel lines of black spots on sides	scattered black freckles on sides	vertical dark blotches on sides

GOGGLE-EYE
Ambloplites rupestris (Rock Bass)

OZARK BASS *Ambloplites constellatus*
SHADOW BASS *Ambloplites ariommus*

Other Names: Shadow Bass (*Ambloplites ariommus*), Ozark Bass (*Ambloplites constellatus*)

Habitat: vegetation on rocky bottoms in clear water lakes and medium-size streams

Range: southern Canada through central and eastern United States to the edge of the Gulf States; Missouri—from the Ozark Region south

Food: crayfish, aquatic insects and small fish

Reproduction: spawns when water temperatures are in the high 60s and 70s; male builds a nest in coarse gravel in shallow water; male guards eggs and fry

Average Size: 8 to 10 inches, 8 ounces to 1 pound

Records: State—2 pounds, 12 ounces, Big Piney River, 1968; North American—3 pounds, York River, Ontario, 1974

Notes: In Missouri the Shadow Bass, the Ozark Bass and the Rock Bass are generally grouped together and known as Goggle-eye. They are all similar in appearance but occupy slightly different habitats. The Rock Bass is a northern fish that may have been introduced to Missouri. The Shadow Bass is a southern fish found in the lower Mississippi River Basin. The Ozark Bass is endemic to the Ozarks, meaning it is originally found only in the Ozark Region of Missouri and Arkansas.

165

Description: dark-green back; dark-olive to bluish sides; yellow to cream belly; scales flecked with yellow, producing a brassy appearance; dark gill spot with pale margin; large mouth with thick lips

Similar Species: Bluegill (pg. 160), Redear Sunfish (pg. 172)

Green Sunfish

dark gill spot has a pale margin

Bluegill

dark gill spot with no clear margin

Redear Sunfish

red-orange margin on gill spot

Green Sunfish

faint blue stripes on head

Redear Sunfish

no blue stripes on head

GREEN SUNFISH

Lepomis cyanellus

Other Names: green perch, sand bass

Habitat: weedy, warm, shallow lakes and backwaters of slow- moving streams

Range: most of the United States into Mexico excluding Florida and the Rocky Mountains; Missouri—abundant statewide

Food: aquatic insects, small crustaceans, fish

Reproduction: male builds nest in less than a foot of weedy water; spawns when water temperatures 60 to 80 degrees; may produce two broods per year; male guards nest and fans eggs until hatching

Average Size: 4 to 6 inches, less than 8 ounces

Records: State—2 pounds, 2 ounces, Stockton Lake, 1971; North American—2 pounds, 2 ounces, Stockton Lake, Missouri, 1971

Notes: Green Sunfish are often mistaken for Bluegills but have a larger mouth and prefer shallower weedbeds. They are very tolerant of turbid water and low oxygen levels, and thrive in warm, weedy lakes and prairie streams. They have become very abundant in some Missouri streams where other sunfish cannot withstand the high turbidity and low oxygen levels. Green Sunfish have a tendency to stunt in small ponds, filling them with small breeding fish. Green Sunfish frequently hybridize with Bluegills producing, large aggressive offspring.

Description: dark greenish-blue back; sides light green and flecked with blue or yellow; belly and chest are bright orange to pale yellow; gill flap tapers into a long, black finger with a red margin

Similar Species: Redear Sunfish (pg. 172)

Longear Sunfish

Redear Sunfish

dark spots on dorsal fin

no spots on dorsal fin

Longear Sunfish

Redear Sunfish

blue green bands on side of head

solid green to bronze head

LONGEAR SUNFISH

Lepomis megalotis

Other Names: Great Lakes longear, blue-and-orange sunfish, red perch

Habitat: clear, moderately weedy, slow-moving shallow streams, and quiet, clear lakes

Range: central states north to Quebec, east to the Appalachian Mountains and as far south as the Gulf of Mexico, introduced into some western states; Missouri— wide-spread in southern half of state

Food: small insects, crustaceans, fish

Reproduction: male builds and guards nest on shallow gravel beds when water temperatures reach the mid-70s

Average Size: 3 to 4 inches, 5 ounces

Records: State—11 ounces, private pond, 2007; North American—1 pound, 12 ounces, Big Round Lake, New Mexico, 1985

Notes: Longears are bright, secretive little sunfish that prefer clear, slow-moving shallow streams, but do well in some clean Missouri lakes. Longears require clear water and do not do well where there is agricultural runoff. Longears readily take still-fished baited hooks but feed on the surface more than other sunfish making them popular with fly fishermen. There is some hybridization between Longears and other sunfish.

Description: blue-green back fading to orange; about 30 orange or red spots on sides of males, brown spots on females; orange pelvic and anal fins; black gill spot with light margin

Similar Species: Redear Sunfish (pg. 172), Longear Sunfish (pg. 168)

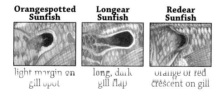

Orangespotted Sunfish — light margin on gill spot

Longear Sunfish — long, dark gill flap

Redear Sunfish — orange or red crescent on gill

ORANGESPOTTED SUNFISH

Lepomis humilis

Other Names: orangespot, dwarf sunfish, pygmy sunfish

Habitat: open to moderately weedy pools with soft bottoms

Range: from the southern Great Lakes through the Mississippi River basin to the Gulf states; Missouri—common statewide

Food: small insects, crustaceans

Reproduction: male builds and guards nest in shallow, weedy water when temperatures reach the mid-60s; colonial nesters with 50 or more nests close together

Average Size: 3 to 4 inches, 4 ounces

Records: none

Notes: This brightly colored sunfish is too small to be an important panfish in Missouri. They tolerate a wide variety of habitats except fast-moving streams. They survive well in silty water and tolerate slight pollution, making them well suited for small lakes in agricultural areas. Orangespotted Sunfish are important as forage for other game fish and may be important for mosquito larvae control in some areas. They make beautiful aquarium fish but may require some live food.

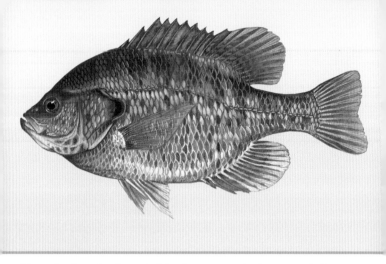

Description: back and sides bronze to dark green, fading to light green; faint vertical bars; bluish stripes on side of head; gill flap short with dark spot and red margin in males

Similar Species: Longear Sunfish (pg. 168), Bluegill (pg. 160)

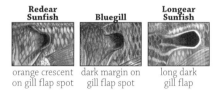

Redear Sunfish
orange crescent on gill flap spot

Bluegill
dark margin on gill flap spot

Longear Sunfish
long dark gill flap

REDEAR SUNFISH

Lepomis microlophus

Other Names: shellcracker, stumpknocker, yellow bream

Habitat: congregates around stumps and logs amid low to moderate vegetation in large, quiet lakes; introduced into farm ponds

Range: northern Midwest through the southern states; introduced into the northern and western states; Missouri—statewide

Food: mainly mollusks

Reproduction: male builds and guards nest in shallow, weedy water in May and June when water temperatures reach the high 60s; may produce second brood well into the summer

Average size: 8 to 10 inches, 8 ounces to 1 pound

Records: State—2 pounds, 7 ounces, Whetstone Creek Conservation Area, 1988; North America—5 pounds, 7$\frac{1}{2}$ ounces, Diversion Canal, South Carolina, 1998

Notes: The Redear Sunfish is a large, highly regarded panfish of the South that is native to southern Missouri and is now stocked throughout the state. The introduction of this large, aggressive sunfish has been very successful and Redears are now one of the most popular panfish in Missouri. Redears prefer warmer water than other Missouri sunfish, and are aggressive feeders in summer but slower to bite in other times of year. Redears feed heavily on snails that attach to vegetation and are best fished for on the outside edge of weedbeds.

173

Description: back dark olive; sides yellow to brassy; scales on sides have light centers forming orange-red or yellow spots, occasionally dark; short ear flap; short rounded pectoral fin

Similar Species: Orangespotted Sunfish (pg. 170), Redear Sunfish (pg. 172)

Redspotted Sunfish	**Orangespotted Sunfish**	**Redspotted Sunfish**	**Redear Sunfish**
spots on single scales	spots cover more than one scale	margin of gill spot yellow or cream	margin of gill spot orange-red

REDSPOTTED SUNFISH

Lepomis miniatus

Other Names: orangespot, dwarf or spotted sunfish, pygmy sunfish, stumpknocker

Habitat: heavily vegetated ponds, lakes swamps and stream pools

Range: Atlantic and Gulf Slope drainages from Carolinas to Texas, lower Mississippi River Basin; Missouri—southeast corner of the state

Food: small insects, crustaceans

Reproduction: male builds and guards nest in shallow, weedy water when temperatures reach the mid-60s; bluish eggs are guarded by males until they hatch

Average Size: 5 to 9 inches, 8 ounces

Records: State—2 ounces, Castor River, 1991; North American—none

Notes: The Redspotted Sunfish is closely related to the Spotted Sunfish, and some consider them subspecies of the same species. The main difference between them is coloration; the spots of eastern sunfish populations are black, and the spots of western populations are red-orange. Redspotted Sunfish prefer warm, weedy water with lots of cover in slow-moving streams and small lakes. They often congregate around stumps and sunken logs. They mostly feed on insects making them easy to catch on crickets or worms. Though frequently caught, Redspotted Sunfish are too small to be an important panfish in Missouri.

175

Description: back and sides greenish gray to brown, lightly mottled with faint vertical bands; stout body; large mouth; red eyes; 3 to 5 reddish-brown streaks radiate from eyes

Similar Species: Bluegill (pg. 160), Green Sunfish (pg. 166) Rock Bass (pg. 164)

Warmouth	**Bluegill**	**Green Sunfish**
jaw extends at least to middle of eye	small mouth does not extend to eye	jaw does not extend to middle of eye

Warmouth	**Rock Bass**
light margin on gill spot	dark gill spot lacks light margin

WARMOUTH

Lepomis gulosus

Centararchadie

Other Names: goggle eye, widemouth sunfish, stump-knocker, weed bass

Habitat: heavy weeds in turbid lakes, swamps and slow-moving streams

Range: southern US from Texas to Florida north to the southern Great Lakes region; Missouri—common in southern and eastern Missouri

Food: crayfish, aquatic insects and small fish

Reproduction: spawns when water temperatures are in the high 60s and 70s; male builds a nest in coarse gravel in submerged vegetation less than 3 feet deep; male guards eggs and fry

Average Size: 11 inches, 8 to 12 ounces

Records: State—1 pound, 4 ounces, private pond, 1984; North American—2 pound, 7 ounces, Yellow River, Florida, 1985

Notes: The Warmouth was historically found only in the southeast corner of Missouri, but has expanded its range to include the southern half of the state and along the Mississippi in the east. Warmouths are solitary, aggressive sight-feeders that are often found near rocks and submerged stumps when not hiding in dense vegetation. They prefer cloudy water with a soft bottom and can withstand low oxygen levels, high silt loads and temperatures into the 90s. Warmouths are small but have a good flavor and are scrappy, strong fighters on light tackle.

177

Description: dark-gray back; bright silver sides with 7 or 8 distinct stripes; two tooth patches; dorsal fin separated, front part hard spines, rear part soft rays

Similar Species: Hybrid Striped Bass (pg. 180), White Bass (pg. 182)

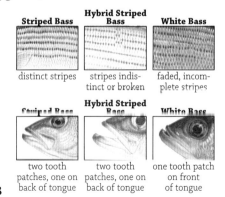

Striped Bass	Hybrid Striped Bass	White Bass
distinct stripes	stripes indistinct or broken	faded, incomplete stripes

Striped Bass	Hybrid Striped Bass	White Bass
two tooth patches, one on back of tongue	two tooth patches, one on back of tongue	one tooth patch on front of tongue

STRIPED BASS

Moronidae

Morone saxatilis

Other Names: striper, streaker, surf bass, rockfish

Habitat: coastal oceans and associated spawning streams; landlocked in some large lakes

Range: the Atlantic coast from Maine to northern Florida, the Gulf Coast from Florida to Texas and introduced to the Pacific coast and some large inland impoundments; Missouri—stocked in large reservoirs, escaped to impounded rivers

Food: small fish

Reproduction: spawns in late spring to early summer in freshwater streams; eggs deposited in riffles at the mouth of large tributaries; eggs must remain suspended to hatch

Average Size: 18 to 30 inches, 10 to 20 pounds

Records: State—56 pounds, 5 ounces, Bull Shoals Lake, 2008; North American—78 pounds, 8 ounces, Atlantic City, New Jersey, 1992

Notes: The Striped Bass is a saltwater fish that migrates into freshwater to spawn. In the early 1960s, it was discovered that Striped Bass could live entirely in freshwater. Large numbers were soon being reared in hatcheries and stocked in many southern and western lakes and rivers. These introduced populations cannot reproduce naturally and must be maintained through stocking. Large numbers of Striped Bass are stocked in Missouri's cool water reservoirs, and they have become a popular sport fish.

Description: dark-gray back; bright silver sides with 7 or 8 indistinct or broken stripes; dorsal fin separated, front part consists of hard spines; rear part consists of soft rays; two tooth patches, one on back of the tongue

Similar Species: Striped Bass (pg. 178), White Bass (pg. 182)

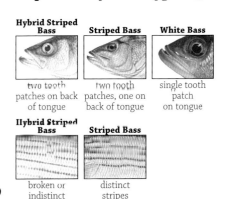

Hybrid Striped Bass
two tooth patches on back of tongue

Striped Bass
two tooth patches, one on back of tongue

White Bass
single tooth patch on tongue

Hybrid Striped Bass
broken or indistinct stripes

Striped Bass
distinct stripes

HYBRID STRIPED BASS

Morone saxatilis X Morone chrysops

Other Names: white striper, wiper

Habitat: open water of large lakes and slow-moving rivers

Range: stocked in about 40 US states; Missouri—stocked in few large reservoirs, it has escaped to rivers below impoundments

Food: small fish

Reproduction: hatchery-produced hybrid that is only occasionally fertile

Average Size: 18 to 20 inches, 8 to 10 pounds

Records: State—20 pounds, 8 ounces, Osage River, 1986; North American—27 pounds, 5 ounces, Greer's Ferry Lake, Arkansas, 1997

Notes: The Striped Bass Hybrid is a hatchery-raised hybrid and most often a cross between a female Striped Bass and a male White Bass. They do not reproduce but may interbreed with the parent stock. Missouri now raises large numbers of fingerlings to stock in impoundments too warm to support Striped Bass. This hard-fighting, tasty bass has now become a favorite with anglers in Missouri and across the country. The Hybrid Striped Bass is also becoming an important aquaculture fish, supplying fillets for the grocery store and the restaurant market.

Description: gray-black back; silver sides with 6 to 8 broken or indistinct stripes; separated dorsal fin; mouth protrudes beyond snout

Similar Species: Hybrid Striped Bass (pg. 180), Striped Bass (pg. 178)

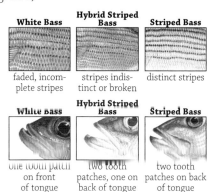

White Bass	Hybrid Striped Bass	Striped Bass
faded, incomplete stripes	stripes indistinct or broken	distinct stripes
White Bass	Hybrid Striped Bass	Striped Bass
one tooth patch on front of tongue	two tooth patches, one on back of tongue	two tooth patches on back of tongue

WHITE BASS

Morone chrysops

Moronidae

Other Names: lake, sand or silver bass, streaker

Habitat: large lakes, rivers and impoundments with relatively clear water

Range: the Great Lakes region to the eastern seaboard, through the southeast to the Gulf and west to Texas; Missouri—statewide

Food: small fish

Reproduction: spawns in late spring or early summer; eggs are spread in open water over gravel beds or rubble 6 to 10 feet deep; some populations migrate to narrow bays or up tributary streams to spawn

Average Size: 18 inches, 8 ounces to 2 pounds

Records: State—5 pounds, 6 ounces, Table Rock Lake, 2002; North American—6 pounds, 7 ounces, Saginaw Bay, Michigan, 1989

Notes: The White Bass is native to Missouri but is much more widespread now than it was historically. This popular fish inhabits wide, deep pools in rivers and open water in large lakes and reservoirs. In lakes, White Bass travel in schools near the surface and can often be spotted by watching for seagulls feeding on baitfish driven to the surface by schools of bass. During the spring spawning run, they are often caught in narrow bays or tributary streams. The flesh is somewhat soft but has a good flavor and can be improved if it is put on ice as soon as the fish are caught.

Description: silvery-yellow to brassy sides with 6 or 7 black stripes broken just above anal fin; yellowish white belly; forked tail; two sections of dorsal fin connected by membrane

Similar Species: Hybrid Striped Bass (pg. 180), Striped Bass (pg. 178), White Bass (pg. 182)

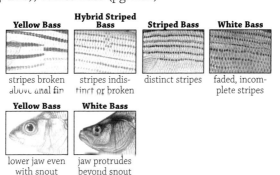

Yellow Bass
stripes broken above anal fin

Hybrid Striped Bass
stripes indistinct or broken

Striped Bass
distinct stripes

White Bass
faded, incomplete stripes

Yellow Bass
lower jaw even with snout

White Bass
jaw protrudes beyond snout

YELLOW BASS

Morone mississippiensis

Other Names: brassy or gold bass, barfish

Habitat: open water over shallow gravel bars in lakes and pools in larger rivers

Range: the Great Lakes region to the eastern seaboard, through the southeast to the Gulf and west to Texas; Missouri—Mississippi River

Food: small fish, insects and crustaceans

Reproduction: spawns in late spring over gravel bars in the mouths of tributary streams

Average Size: 8 to 12 inches, 8 ounces to 1 pound

Records: State—9 ounces, Sandy Slough, 1995, North American—2 pounds, 8 ounces, Tennessee River, Alabama, 2000

Notes: The Yellow Bass is a close cousin to the White Bass. In Missouri Yellow Bass are primarily found in the Mississippi River. Its schooling and feeding habits are similar to the White Bass, but it tends to stay in the middle of the water column or near the bottom. The Yellow Bass is a popular panfish in some areas where its flaky, white flesh is considered superior to that of White Bass. In Missouri they are occasionally caught by river fishermen, but they are too rare to be of much interest to most anglers.

Description: olive to blackish green back; silver-green sides with no stripes; front spiny dorsal fin is connected by a small membrane to the soft ray back portion

Similar Species: Striped Bass (pg. 178), Striped Bass Hybrid (pg. 180), White Bass (pg. 182)

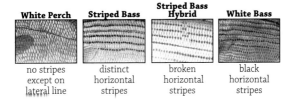

White Perch	Striped Bass	Striped Bass Hybrid	White Bass
no stripes except on lateral line	distinct horizontal stripes	broken horizontal stripes	black horizontal stripes

WHITE PERCH

Morone americana

Other Names: narrow-mouth bass, silver or sea perch

Habitat: brackish water in coastal areas; near-shore areas of the Great Lakes; expanding range into smaller freshwater lakes and rivers

Range: the Mississippi River drainage south to the Gulf of Mexico, Atlantic coast from Maine to South Carolina; Missouri—Mississippi and Missouri Rivers

Food: fish eggs, minnows, insects, crustaceans

Reproduction: spawns in late spring over gravel bars of tributary streams

Average Size: 6 to 8 inches, 1 pound or less

Records: State—open; North American—4 pounds, 12 ounces, Messalonskee Lake, Maine, 1949

Notes: The White Perch is a brackish-water fish native to the coastal Atlantic states. White Perch became established in some large eastern reservoirs after making spawning runs up freshwater tributary streams. The White Perch's range is now quickly expanding into many freshwater habitats, often appearing in places where it is unwanted. They are now increasingly common in the Mississippi and Missouri Rivers. It is a very popular panfish in some regions and hated in others. The flesh is firm and white with a good flavor.

GLOSSARY

adipose fin a small, fleshy fin without rays, located on the midline of the fish's back between the dorsal fin and the tail

air bladder a balloon-like organ located in the gut area of a fish, used to control buoyancy—and in the respiration of some species such as gar; also called "swim bladder" or "gas bladder"

anadromous a fish that hatches in freshwater, migrates to the ocean, then re-enters streams or rivers from the sea (or large inland body of water) to spawn

anal fin a single fin located on the underside near the tail

anterior toward the front of a fish, opposite of posterior

bands horizontal markings running lengthwise along the side of a fish

barbel thread-like sensory structures on a fish's head often near the mouth, commonly called "whiskers"; used for taste or smell

bars vertical markings on the side of a fish

brood swarm a large group or "cloud" of young fish such as Black Bullheads

carnivore a species that subsists on animal flesh

catadromous a fish that lives in freshwater and migrates into saltwater to spawn, such as the American Eel

caudal fin the tail or tail fin

caudal peduncle the portion of the fish's body located between the anal fin and the beginning of the tail

crustacean a crayfish, water flea, crab or other animal belonging to group of mostly aquatic species that have paired antennae, jointed legs and an exterior skeleton (exoskeleton); common food for many fish

dorsal relating to the top of the fish, on or near the back; opposite of the ventral, or lower, part of the fish

dorsal fin the fin or fins located along the top of a fish's back

exotic a foreign species not native to a watershed, such as the Zebra Mussel

fingerling a juvenile fish, generally 1 to 10 inches in length, in its first year of life

fork length the overall length of fish from the mouth to the deepest part of the tail notch

fry recently hatched young fish that have already absorbed their yolk sacs

game fish a species regulated by laws for recreational fishing

gills organs used in aquatic respiration (breathing)

gill cover large bone covering the fish's gills, also called opercle or operculum

gill flap also called ear flap; fleshy projection on the back edge of the gill cover of some fish such as Bluegill

gill raker a comb-like projection from the gill arch

ichthyologist a scientist who studies fish

invertebrates animals without backbones, such as insects, leeches and earthworms

kype hooked jaw acquired by some trout and salmon mainly during breeding season

lateral line a series of pored scales along the side of a fish that contain organs used to detect vibrations

mandible lower jaw

mollusk an invertebrate with a smooth, soft body such as a clam or a snail, often having an outer shell

native an indigenous or naturally occurring species

omnivore a fish or animal that eats plants and animal matter

otolith calcium concentration found in the inner ear of fish; used to determine age of some fish; also called ear bone

opercle the bone covering the gills, also called the gill cover or operculum

panfish small freshwater game fish that can be fried whole in a pan, such as Black Crappie, Bluegill and Yellow Perch

pectoral fins paired fins on the side of the fish located just behind the gills

pelvic fins paired fins located below or behind the pectoral fins on the bottom (ventral portion) of the fish

plankton floating or weakly swimming aquatic plants and animals, including larval fish, that drift with the current; often eaten by fish; individual organisms are called plankters

range the geographic region in which a species is found

ray, hard stiff fin support; resembles a spine but is jointed

ray, soft flexible fin support, sometimes branched

redd a nest-like depression made by a male or female fish during spawning, often refers to nest of trout and salmon species

roe fish eggs

scales small, flat plates covering the outer skin of many fish

spawning the process of fish reproduction; involves females laying eggs and males fertilizing them to produce young fish

spine stiff, non-jointed structures found along with soft rays in some fins

spiracle an opening on the posterior portion of the head above and behind the eye

standard length length of the fish from the mouth to the end of the vertebral column

substrate bottom composition of a lake, stream or river

subtenninal mouth a mouth below the snout of the fish

swim bladder see air bladder

terminal mouth forward-facing

total length length of fish from the mouth to the tail compressed to its fullest length

tributary a stream that feeds into another stream, river or lake

turbid cloudy; water clouded by suspended sediments or plant matter that limits visibility and the passage of light

vent the opening at the end of the digestive tract

ventral the underside of the fish

vertebrate an animal with a backbone

zooplankton the animal component of plankton, tiny animals that float or swim weakly; common food for small fish

PRIMARY REFERENCES

Becker, G. C.
Fishes of Wisconsin
University of Wisconsin Press, 1983

Lee, D. S. et al.
Atlas of North American Freshwater Fishes
North Carolina State Museum of Natural History, 1980

McClane, A. J.
Freshwater Fishes of North America
Henry Holt and Company, 1978

Page, L. M. and Burr, B. M.
Freshwater Fishes, Peterson Field Guide
Houghton Mifflin Company, 1991

Pflieger, W. L.
The Fishes of Missouri
Conservation Commission of the State of Missouri, 1997

Smith, P. W.
The Fish of Illinois
University of Illinois Press, 1979

INDEX

194

ABOUT THE AUTHOR

Dave Bosanko was born in Kansas and studied engineering before following his love of nature to degrees in biology and chemistry from Emporia State University. He spent thirty years as staff biologist at two of the University of Minnesota's field stations. Though his training was in mammal physiology, Dave worked on a wide range of research projects ranging from fish, bird and mammal population studies to experiments with biodiversity and prairie restoration. A lifelong fisherman and avid naturalist, he is now spending his retirement writing, fishing and traveling.